COLLECTING
FROM STOCK

C W HILL

GRANADA
London Toronto Sydney New York

Granada Publishing Limited
Frogmore, St Albans, Herts AL2 2NF
and
3 Upper James Street, London W1R 4BP
866 United Nations Plaza, New York, NY 10017, USA
117 York Street, Sydney, NSW 2000, Australia
100 Skyway Avenue, Toronto, Ontario, Canada M9W 3A6
PO Box 84165, Greenside, 2034 Johannesburg, South Africa
61 Beach Road, Auckland, New Zealand

Published by Granada in 1980
Hardback ISBN 0 246 11324 3
Paperback ISBN 0 583 30387 0

Copyright © C W Hill 1980

Typeset by Georgia Origination, Liverpool

Printed and bound in Hong Kong by
Wing King Tong Co Ltd

Granada®
Granada Publishing®

Contents

Acknowledgements

My acknowledgements are due, and gratefully tendered, to Olive Portsmouth and David Couldridge for their constant encouragement in my numismatic work and to my wife, Janet Hill, for her meticulous preparation of my manuscript.

The publishers are grateful to the following for supplying photos of coins or for lending coins to be photographed: the author; Stanley Gibbons Currency Ltd.; *Coins* magazine; British Museum (photos Ray Gardner) and Marianne Taylor.

Photos of coins being minted are from the Central Office of Information.

Collecting Coins

Introduction

To the question 'Why do you collect coins?' there are several answers, because different people become collectors for different reasons. Most people collect coins for their historical interest. When a collector holds in his hand a Roman denarius, the ancestor of our modern penny, he soon feels his imagination stirring at the thought of the centuries of history that have passed since Roman craftsmen designed and minted the tiny silver coin. What tales the denarius might have to tell, if only it could speak!

Other people choose to collect the coins of a favourite country, perhaps the one in which they live or in which they have spent happy holidays. The coins make attractive souvenirs, illustrating the country's history, portraying its celebrated men and women or featuring its wildlife, its famous buildings and national monuments.

Some collectors are attracted to coins simply by the pictures on them. A large and interesting collection can easily be formed, for example, of coins which feature ships in their designs. Other popular themes for a collection include horsemen on coins, the story of exploration in Africa or Australasia, Queens on coins and national coats-of-arms.

Collectors who are interested in science and technology may like to form a collection illustrating the different methods of making coins, from primitive hammering by hand-tools to mass production by modern machinery. A study of the different metals used for coinage might make an informative collection for anyone planning a career in metallurgy.

Most collectors, especially in these days of rapid inflation, look upon their coins as a sound investment. If the collector has chosen his coins wisely and carefully, he may be able to sell them for appreciably more than they originally cost him. Gold and silver coins, in particular, have increased steadily in value during the past ten or fifteen years. Even coins in the base metals such as copper, bronze and nickel may be worth more than their original prices.

These are some of the main reasons why so many people of all ages are coin collectors. The purpose of this book is to suggest the best ways of forming a coin collection, to tell some of the interesting stories that lie behind familiar coins, and to show how to get the maximum pleasure and profit from collecting coins.

1
Coins of
Early Times

Before coins were invented, people had to use a system of barter for buying and selling goods. A man who grew olives might offer a jar of his olive oil in exchange for a pair of sandals from the sandal-maker. A weaver might exchange a length of cloth for a new cooking-pot made by the blacksmith. Difficulties arose when the man with olive oil to spare found that the sandal-maker already had sufficient for his needs and would exchange his sandals only for a piece of leather or a sack of flour.

Some articles were more popular for bartering than others. Cattle were almost always acceptable because they provided meat and milk. Leather, in the form of ox-hides, was another popular commodity because it had so many uses in making footwear, clothing, harness and even drinking vessels. But an ox was too valuable to be used for a small purchase and an ox-hide might be ruined if it had to be cut into pieces for making small payments.

Such difficulties led people in the Mediterranean countries about four thousand years ago to introduce a primitive system of currency. This consisted of copper or bronze replicas of an ox-hide, curling at the edges and marked on one side to represent hair, just as if they were made of real hide. Known as talents, from a Greek word meaning a weight, these replicas were in various sizes, some weighing as much as ½cwt (25 kilos). A number of them have been found in Greece and there is no doubt that they were intended to simplify the complicated system of barter. A man would accept a bronze talent in payment for the goods he was selling because he knew that he, in his turn, could exchange it later for goods he wanted to buy from someone else.

The next step in the invention of coins as we know them came about the middle of the 7th century BC in the kingdom of Lydia, in Asia Minor, now part of Turkey. Writing about two hundred years later, the Greek historian Herodotus recorded that the Lydians 'were the first men whom we know to have minted and used gold and silver coins'.

Lydia was a prosperous kingdom and its capital, Sardis, was an important centre of trade between the countries of the eastern Mediterranean and those stretching further east through Babylonia and Persia to India. For international trade such as this, barter was unsuitable. To simplify it, Lydian merchants began stamping small pieces of precious metal with devices such as a lion's head or a pattern of squares. The metal they used was electrum, a mixture of silver and gold, and the coins were simply round or oval lumps resembling tiny pebbles. Only a few of these Lydian coins have been discovered but it is clear that the merchants who issued them would recognise them by the devices stamped on them and would readily accept them in exchange for goods.

About 560 BC a king named Croesus succeeded to the throne of Lydia. He ordered that instead of being made of electrum, in which the amounts of gold and silver varied considerably, all Lydian coins should be minted in either pure gold or pure silver. These are the coins of which Herodotus wrote. Unfortunately Croesus unwisely embroiled his country in a war with Persia. The Persians defeated his army, captured Croesus himself and conquered Lydia. But stories of his enormous wealth have persisted and even today we sometimes speak of a very wealthy person as being 'as rich as Croesus'.

The Lydian example was soon copied in neighbouring countries and the Greek city states began to issue coins of their own. One of the first to do so was the island of Aegina, which lies about twenty miles off-shore from Athens. The Aegina coins were round silver coins called staters depicting a turtle on one side and a geometric pattern on the other (*Figure 1*). Although to modern eyes they seem to be crudely made and uneven in shape, the 'turtles', as the coins were called, were accepted throughout the Greek islands as a standard coinage of good quality. Some have even been found in hoards of coins buried in the Nile Delta, in Egypt, where they may have been used by merchants from Aegina to pay for Egyptian corn, linen or glassware.

Other Greek states chose different devices for their coins. Those of Athens had on one side a portrait of the goddess Athena, after

1 Silver stater known as 'turtle'

whom the city was named, and on the other an owl symbolising the wisdom for which the goddess was renowned. All the silver coins of Corinth have a picture of Pegasus, the winged horse of Greek mythology, and many coins minted in the city of Argos have a capital A in their design.

Some of the most attractive of the ancient Greek coins are those issued in the Greek colonies in Sicily and southern Italy. Syracuse, founded about 735 BC by settlers from Corinth, was the most important city in Sicily and its coins reflected its prosperity. Many had a portrait of Arethusa, one of the sea-nymphs, with dolphins swimming round her (*Figure 2*). A young man riding on a dolphin

2 Silver tetradrachm

3 Silver stater minted in Thurium, southern Italy

4 Silver tetradrachm of King Philip II of Macedon showing Zeus

can be seen on coins from the Greek colony of Tarentum, now the city of Taranto, because its founder, Taras, was said to have been saved from shipwreck by a dolphin which took him on its back safely to shore. A silver stater minted about 430 BC in Thurium depicted a bull (*Figure 3*).

Alexander the Great, who had conquered so many countries in eastern Europe and Asia, died in 323 BC and his vast empire was divided among his generals. To assert their authority they began to replace the portraits of gods and goddesses (*Figure 4*), which had been on the coins, by portraits of Alexander and later by portraits of themselves. One who did so was Ptolemy, who became the ruler of Egypt and founded a dynasty which lasted for almost three hundred years. Among the monarchs portrayed on Egyptian coins were Ptolemy himself, his daughter, Queen Arsinoe, and the celebrated Queen Cleopatra, who was one of his descendants.

Most of the ancient Greek coins were made of silver but there were also a few gold coins and some of bronze. All the gold coins are rare and valuable. The large silver coins, known as tetradrachms, usually cost at least £100 in fine condition and rare examples are worth much more. Some of the small bronze coins may be bought at prices between about £10 and £50 each in fine or very fine condition.

When we speak of someone as being 'impecunious' we mean that he or she has no money. The adjective is derived from the Latin word *pecunia*, meaning money, and this in turn was derived from another Latin word, *pecus*, which means cattle. This close connection between cattle and wealth, for a man who had large herds of cattle was likely to be very wealthy, is illustrated by the earliest Roman coins. Soon after the Greeks had begun making their copper or bronze replicas of ox-hides to serve as a coinage instead of barter, the Romans also began making rectangular slabs of bronze bearing devices such as a bull, a pig; an ear of corn and a anchor. These slabs were used in buying and selling but because they weighed up to about 5lbs (2½ kilos), they were cumbersome and inconvenient.

After about 270 BC the bronze slabs were gradually replaced by circular bronze coins. Most of these weighed about ¼lb (100 grams) but some were lighter and others were much heavier. Like the Greek coins, they had no inscriptions but their designs sometimes portrayed Roman gods, among them Mars, the god of war, and Apollo, the sun-god, or featured various devices, an acorn, a scallop shell or ears of corn.

As Rome grew wealthier and more powerful, the primitive bronze coinage proved inadequate, so that gold and silver coins were introduced. A mint employing over two hundred workmen was established near the Colosseum, in Rome. The Roman government, the Senate, appointed three officials to supervise not only the Rome mint but also the mints which were opened in other cities in the Roman Empire. This central control of the coinage meant that an easily identifiable and standardised series of coins could circulate wherever the Empire extended.

The series consisted of gold, silver and bronze or copper coins. The principal of these were a gold aureus, a silver denarius and a sestertius, dupondius and as, all made of bronze and copper. The silver denarius, about the same size as the modern British decimal penny, was the key coin in the series, equal to 4 sestertii, 8 dupondii or 16 copper asses. The gold aureus, seldom seen by ordinary citizens, was worth 25 denarii. These coins were as readily accepted by a shopkeeper in Rome as by a merchant in Alexandria, an innkeeper in Tarragona or a legionary guarding Hadrian's Wall in the far north of Britain. The Roman coinage was, with the system of laws and the well-ordered government, one of the great benefits of Roman rule.

For the first few centuries of its rise to power Rome was a republic. It was governed by two magistrates, the Consuls, who were elected each year by the most important citizens. The Consuls were advised by the Senate, whose three hundred members held office for life. The republican coins had portraits of gods and goddesses on one side, the obverse. Apollo, Mars, Ceres, the goddess of the harvest, and Hercules, the celebrated strong man of Greek and Roman mythology, were popular choices. On the other side, the reverse, the coins often showed a charioteer furiously driving a four-horse chariot, known as a quadriga, or the more tranquil scene of a farmer ploughing with two yoked oxen.

The Roman republic came to an end during the half-century before the birth of Jesus Christ. A struggle for power among three ambitious generals, Pompey, Julius Caesar and Octavian, ended with the murder of Pompey in Egypt in 48 BC and of Julius Caesar in the Senate House at Rome in 44 BC, leaving Octavian to become sole ruler. He took the title of Emperor Augustus and very soon ordered the issue of coins bearing his new name and his portrait.

The following two centuries were the most glorious in Roman history. Each succeeding emperor was portrayed on the coins that circulated throughout the Empire. Round the portrait were inscribed in neat, clear lettering the names and titles of the emperor, usually abbreviated to fit the space available. The following are the commonest abbreviations, with their meanings:

On the coin	In full	Meaning
AUG	AUGUSTUS	The usual title of the Emperor
CAES	CAESAR	The name inherited from the family of Julius Caesar
CENS PER	CENSOR PERPETUUS	Censor, or Chief Magistrate, for life
COS	CONSUL	The Emperor was usually also a Consul
IMP	IMPERATOR	Head of the armed forces
P M	PONTIFEX MAXIMUS	Head of the Roman religion, or High Priest
P P	PATER PATRIAE	Father of his country

| S C | SENATUS CONSULTO | By permission or by decree of the Senate |
| TRIB P | TRIBUNICIA POTESTAS | Holder of the power of the Tribunes, or representatives of the people |

The reverses of Roman coins were frequently used by the emperors to publicise their achievements, the victories won by their armies, the new provinces added to the Empire or new buildings erected in Rome. In AD 132 a Jewish rebellion broke out against Roman rule in Judaea. By the time the rebellion was finally crushed, more than three years later, the province had been devastated. The Emperor Hadrian at once gave orders for the city of Jerusalem to be rebuilt and for the temple of Jupiter, which had already replaced the Jewish Temple, to be renovated and re-opened. Special bronze sestertii, issued to illustrate the Emperor's generosity, showed his portrait on one side and, on the other, a symbolic scene. The Emperor is standing erect and holding out a hand to help a kneeling woman to her feet. Around them are grouped three small children holding palm-leaves, the symbols of peace. So that everyone seeing the sestertii should understand their meaning, the name IUDAEA is inscribed below the scene.

Hadrian is best known in British history for the wall which he ordered to be built from the Tyne to the Solway Firth to protect the Roman province of Britain from the attacks of the fierce Picts. The Emperor visited Britain in AD 122, probably to inspect the site where the wall was to be built. Soon afterwards the mint in Rome produced special bronze asses to commemorate the visit. His portrait appeared, as usual, on the obverse. The reverse showed a woman seated on a pile of stones, with a shield at her side and a spear or a long sceptre in her hand. In the lower part of the design was the name of the province which the seated woman personified, Britannia (*Figure 5*). This was her first appearance on coins and she can still be seen on British 50p coins today.

The Roman designers were particularly adept at depicting views and crowd scenes, even in the tiny space of a coin. On the reverse of a bronze sestertius, minted about AD 55 for the Emperor Nero, there is a bird's eye view of the harbour at Ostia, the port for

5 Bronze coin showing Emperor Hadrian (*obverse*), Britannia (*reverse*)

6 Bronze sestertius showing Emperor Antoninus Pius

Rome. At the top of the picture is a lighthouse with a statue of Neptune holding the light. Grouped in front of it are seven ships of various sizes and in one of them two sailors are busy on deck, one apparently unfurling the sails and the other hoisting the anchor. Ostia stands at the mouth of the River Tiber, so the foreground of the picture is occupied by the reclining figure of a bearded man representing 'Father Tiber'. All this can clearly be seen on a coin that measures less than 1½ ins (38 mms) in diameter.

Hadrian and his successors, Antoninus Pius (*Figure 6*) and Marcus Aurelius, were firm and capable rulers but even before Marcus Aurelius died in AD 180, the Roman Empire was beginning to weaken. Enemies were threatening the frontiers of many distant provinces and a succession of selfish and incompetent emperors hastened the decline. To save money for the imperial treasury, the weight of the gold coins was reduced and the amount of silver in the denarii was cut by half, the deficiency being made up by increasing the copper in the alloy. When people protested, a new silver coin, the antoninianus, was introduced but this too was steadily debased until by about AD 270 it contained 95% bronze and only 5% silver. As a last resort the Emperor Diocletian introduced yet another coin, the follis, which was made of bronze coated with a thin wash

7 Emperor Constantine follis

8 a) Sestertius of Emperor Nero (*obverse & reverse*),

b) Sestertius of Emperor Galba, (*reverse*)

of silver (*Figure 7*). Like the Roman Empire itself, the splendid Roman coinage had become only a shadow of its former self.

Although they were minted almost two thousand years ago, Roman coins were produced in such large numbers that many are still comparatively common. It is possible to buy examples of the bronze sestertius in reasonable condition for less than £1. The silver denarius is more expensive and all Roman gold coins are scarce and valuable. Also scarce are the coins of emperors whose reigns were short. During AD 238 no fewer than five emperors followed one another in rapid succession, so that their coins were minted in small numbers and are now rare. The coins of emperors such as Tiberius (AD 14 to 37), Nero (54 to 68) (*Figure 8a*), Domitian (81 to 96) and Hadrian (117 to 138) are cheaper because many more were minted and have survived (*Figure 8b*).

2

Two Thousand Years
of British Coins

When Julius Caesar was conquering Gaul, the country we now know as north-eastern France, he found that the Celtic people living there had been helped in their resistance to the Roman invasion by Celts living across the narrow seas in southern Britain. This, and a desire to explore the little-known island, prompted Julius Caesar to lead an expedition to Britain in 55 BC. His first attempt showed him that the native tribes could not be conquered easily and he returned for a second attempt the following year. Soon afterwards Julius Caesar became involved in the struggle for power in Rome, so the conquest of Britain was not completed.

Writing later of his war in Gaul, Caesar recorded that the Britons 'used copper or copper coins or bars of iron, carefully made to a certain weight, as money'. This was only part of the truth, for we know from hoards that have been found that the Celts on both sides of the Channel had also been using gold and silver coins for at least a century before Caesar came to Britain.

The coins were very strange. They were crudely made copies of ancient Greek coins which had been minted some two hundred years previously. Craftsmen in Gaul had apparently made copies of the Greek coins and British craftsmen had later made copies from these copies. As a result the designs had become almost unrecognisable. The portrait of Apollo on the Greek coins deteriorated into a meaningless jumble of dots and squiggles. An ear of wheat looked like a fishbone and the spirited horses drawing the chariot on the Greek coins became a single emaciated nag hardly recognisable as a horse (*Figure 9*). Until recent years these Celtic staters were very rare but many more examples have been discovered by treasure hunters using metal detectors. So primitive are the designs that treasure hunters have sometimes failed to recognise their finds as being coins.

9 A rare gold Celtic stater

In AD 43 the Romans made a more determined effort to conquer Britain and for almost four hundred years much of the country was a Roman province. The Romans introduced their own coinage and later established a mint in London. There may also have been mints at other places in Britain, probably Colchester and the Roman naval bases of Richborough, in Kent, and Bitterne, near Southampton, but this is not known for certain.

As well as the coins featuring Britannia, mentioned in Chapter 1, other coins were issued to commemorate the victories of several emperors over rebellious British tribes. When barbarians from the north overran Hadrian's Wall in AD 197, for example, the Emperor Septimius Severus came in person to lead the re-conquest of northern Britain. As soon as the barbarians had been defeated, the mint in Rome issued special coins to announce the Emperor's success. VICTORIAE BRIT. - 'Victories in Britannia' - was their triumphant inscription.

Despite their early successes the Romans were eventually forced to give way before the attacks of barbarians on all their outlying provinces. In AD 410 the last Roman legion in Britain was recalled to help in the defence of Rome itself. This left the native Celtic chieftains to quarrel among themselves. One of them foolishly invited mercenaries from northern Germany to fight for him against his rivals. The newcomers found southern Britain much to their liking and soon more of them were arriving to settle in Britain.

These Angles, Saxons and Jutes were neither such skilled craftsmen nor such capable administrators as the Romans. They were mainly farmers and forest dwellers, so they re-introduced the old system of barter, supplemented by small, crudely minted silver coins. Their designs were roughly copied from those of the Roman coins still in circulation but with the spread of Christianity a cross was often included in the reverse design. In the south of England the Anglo-Saxon coins were known as sceats but in the northern kingdom of Northumbria, where the coins were usually made of copper, they were known as stycas. Apart from the coins issued by the Anglo-Saxon kingdoms into which Britain had been divided, coins were also produced by the archbishops of Canterbury and York.

About AD 770 two little-known kings of Kent copied the silver deniers which were being used in the kingdom of the Franks, the country we now know as France. These deniers were larger and better made than the sceats. A few years later the powerful King Offa also ordered similar coins to be minted in his Midland kingdom of Mercia, and they were quickly introduced in the other Anglo-Saxon kingdoms, East Anglia, Northumbria and Wessex (*Figures 10a*, *b*, *c*, *d*). Even when the Vikings crossed the North Sea

a) King Offa,

b) King Alfred,

c) King Edward the Elder

10 Silver pennies

d) King Edward the Confessor

from Norway and Denmark, first to raid and then to settle in England, they were content to copy the Anglo-Saxon silver coins, which came to be known as pennies.

There is a bewildering range of designs among the Anglo-Saxon and Viking pennies, partly because they were issued by so many kings and archbishops, but mainly because they were made at so many mints. Their inscriptions usually gave the name of the ruler for whom they were being issued, the name of the moneyer who produced them, and the name or abbreviation of the town where the mint was located. During the reign of Ethelred the Unready (978-1016), for example, mints in more than seventy English towns, among them Aylesbury, Totnes and Taunton, were making coins. About seventy mints, including those at Pershore, Worcester and Stafford, made coins for Edward the Confessor (1042-1066). Even during the brief reign of the last Anglo-Saxon king, Harold, about forty mints, including Bedford, Derby and Warwick, were able to mint coins bearing his portrait.

A great deal still remains to be discovered about the coinage of Anglo-Saxon England. Some coins are known only from single examples, while others were minted in large numbers and may be bought from dealers at prices from about £25 or £30 each if in fine condition, less if badly worn.

After Duke William of Normandy had defeated King Harold at the battle of Hastings and made himself King of England, he quickly began making changes in his new kingdom. He confiscated the lands of Anglo-Saxon noblemen to give to his own Norman knights and he replaced the Anglo-Saxon bishops by Normans. But he made few changes in the coinage. He continued to have the silver pennies minted, replacing the portrait of King Harold by his own, but continuing to have a cross as the main feature of the reverse design. As we know from their names on the coins, William even employed the same craftsmen, the moneyers, who had minted coins for the last Anglo-Saxon kings (*Figure 11*).

The Norman and Plantagenet monarchs who followed William the Conqueror also issued similar silver pennies. Anyone who wanted small change simply cut a penny into two halfpennies or four farthings, using the cross on the reverse as a guide. Because the cross was quite small these coins of the 11th, 12th and early 13th centuries were known as Short Cross pennies (*Figure 12*).

11 William the Conqueror silver penny

12 Henry II short cross penny

As the coins had no milling round the rim, it was unusual to find a perfectly circular coin. The irregular shape provided a tempting opportunity for unscupulous people to snip tiny shavings of metal from the edge of a coin before passing it on. By collecting the snippets of silver and melting them down, a dishonest person could make a handsome profit.

In 1247, in an effort to prevent the clipping of coins, King Henry III (1216-1272) ordered that the cross on the reverse should be extended so that the arms reached to the edge of the coin. Any clipping would then be easily noticed. The new coins were known as Long Cross pennies (*Figure 13*). Henry III also introduced a large

13 Henry III long cross penny

gold penny valued at twenty silver pence but this coin proved unpopular and very few were minted. Another of the King's innovations was to have the Latin numeral III or the word TERCI inscribed after his name on the Long Cross pennies, to show that he was the third English king of that name.

The next king, Edward I (1272-1307) also improved the coinage. He issued tiny silver farthings and halfpennies, and introduced a new coin, a large silver groat, which was worth fourpence (*Figure 14*). By this time trade between England and her European neighbours was expanding rapidly, particularly in woollen cloth, linen, wines and glassware. The English coinage was proving inadequate for wealthy merchants trading in expensive commodities, so in 1344 King Edward III (1327-1377) introduced a series of gold coins. The first were a florin valued at 72 silver pence, a half-florin, also known as a leopard because this animal was depicted on the obverse, and a quarter-florin. These were soon replaced by even

14 Edward I silver groat

15 a) Edward III gold noble (*reverse*)   b) Edward IV gold noble (*reverse*)

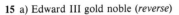

16 Henry VII gold sovereign

17 Henry VII silver testoon or shilling

18 Philip & Mary silver shilling

19 Elizabeth I shilling

larger gold coins, a noble valued at eighty silver pence, a half-noble and a quarter-noble. They were all in elaborate designs, the noble and half-noble showing the King in a ship (*Figure 15*), and the quarter-noble bearing the coats-of-arms of England and France, as the English kings claimed to be rulers of France also.

Later monarchs made minor changes and additions to the coinage. Among the new coins introduced during the 15th century were a large gold rose-noble, also known as a ryal, with half-ryals and quarter-ryals, and a small gold angel and half-angel. The rose-noble was given its name because it had a rose in the reverse design. The angel derived its name from the picture of the Archangel Michael on the obverse. The illustration shows a gold sovereign with a rose incorporated in the reverse design (*Figure 16*).

Another interesting coin, introduced by King Henry VII (1485-1509) was a silver twelve-pence piece. This was at first called a testoon, from the Italian word *testa*, meaning a head, because it had a portrait of the King as its obverse design. It later became known as a shilling and it has remained one of the most useful British coins, surviving today as the 5p piece (*Figures 17, 18, 19*).

Some monarchs tried to make extra profit for the royal treasury by debasing the silver coins, reducing the amount of silver in them and replacing it by a cheaper metal, usually copper. One who did so was King Henry VIII (1509-1547). Some of his coins had a full face portrait in which his nose was the most prominent feature (*Figure 20*). So poor was the quality of the silver that when the coins had been in circulation for a short time, the nose acquired a coppery shine. As a result people jokingly called the King 'Old Copper-nose'.

20 Henry VIII shilling

21 Edward VI silver crown

During the short reign of the young King Edward VI (1547-1553) four new silver coins, a crown, halfcrown, sixpence and threepence, were added to the series. For the first time, also, the date of issue was inscribed on some of the coins. The shillings minted in 1548 were dated in Roman numerals MDXLVIII and the crowns minted in 1551 had the date in the ordinary Arabic numerals (*Figure 21*).

The main deficiency in the coinage was the lack of small change. During the reign of Queen Elizabeth I (1558-1603) an effort was made to solve this problem by issuing silver three-farthing coins but these, measuring only about half an inch (13 mms) in diameter, were too tiny to be convenient. The Queen's successor, King James I (1603-1625) decided that the answer was to issue copper farthings which would be larger than silver coins because copper was a cheaper metal. Instead of ordering the Royal Mint to produce the farthings, the King awarded the contract for minting them to one of his friends, Lord Harrington, of Exton, in Rutland. The King would not allow his portrait to appear on such insignificant coins but he did insist on a share of Lord Harrington's profits from the transaction.

The Civil War between King Charles I and his Parliament brought chaos to the kingdom and to the coinage. Support for the Parliament was strongest in London and the south-east of England, so that the Roundheads controlled the Royal Mint, which was in the Tower of London. Because the King needed money to pay his soldiers, he appealed to his supporters, the Cavaliers, to donate

22 Charles I siege coin

their gold and silver plate, including dishes, jugs, candlesticks and other valuables, to be melted down for minting into coins. Even the Oxford colleges were firmly persuaded to give their prized possessions to the royal cause.

To produce the new coins, the King ordered mints to be established at Shrewsbury, Oxford and Bristol. Other towns where coins were also made for short periods included Truro, Exeter, Chester and Worcester. Because the King was short of gold, he introduced huge one-pound coins made of silver. Showing the King on horseback with sword in hand, these coins measured more than two inches (50 mms) in diameter. In some towns where Cavalier forces were besieged by the Roundheads, the garrison coined its own money by cutting silver plate into small pieces and stamping them with a value, the name or initial letters of the town and a royal crown or similar device. Some of the coins were round but others were diamond-shaped or roughly octagonal (*Figure 22*). Known as obsidional pieces, from the Latin word *obsidio*, meaning a siege, the coins were issued in Carlisle, Newark, Pontefract and Scarborough. Most types are now very rare.

Meanwhile the Royal Mint in the Tower of London continued to produce coins with the name and portrait of King Charles I. This was intended to show that despite their quarrel with him the Roundheads recognised that he was the lawful monarch. Only after the King had been executed in 1649 did the Mint begin to make coins in new designs showing St. George's Cross and the inscription THE COMMONWEALTH OF ENGLAND. A few coins with a

23 Silver coin showing Oliver Cromwell as Lord Protector

portrait of the Lord Protector, Oliver Cromwell, were also minted (*Figure 23*).

With the restoration of King Charles II to the throne in 1660, several changes in the British coinage were planned. Most important was the introduction in 1663 of a new gold coin, the guinea, followed by larger 2-guinea and 5-guinea pieces. The name of the new coin was derived from that part of West Africa, the Guinea Coast, where much of the gold for the coins was obtained by the Royal Africa Company. At first the guinea was reckoned as equal to twenty shillings but the value changed several times as the price of gold rose or fell. It was eventually decided, in 1717, to fix the value of the guinea at twenty-one shillings (*Figure 24*).

At the other end of the scale the Royal Mint at last made an effort to provide the small change which had been lacking for so long. In 1672 the first regal halfpennies and farthings were introduced. They had a portrait of King Charles II on the obverse, while on the reverse the figure of Britannia re-appeared after an

24 Charles II guinea

absence of fifteen centuries. Since 1672 she has been featured regularly on British coins.

For the greater part of the 18th century there were few changes in the coinage. Britain was almost continuously at war with France and usually with Spain also. In 1702 a combined British and Dutch attack on the Spanish port of Vigo led to the capture of a large quantity of gold and silver brought by Spanish ships from Mexico and South America. Much of this treasure was sent to the Royal Mint to be made into coins. To commemorate the British part in the victory the name VIGO was inscribed below the portrait of Queen Anne on the gold and silver coins minted from the captured treasure.

A similar event occurred in the reign of King George II (1727-1760). During a round-the-world voyage in the early 1740s, the British admiral Lord Anson captured a Spanish ship homeward bound from Mexico and laden with treasure. More treasure was captured by two British ships which attacked a French convoy sailing home with treasure from Peru. Again some of the gold and silver was sent to the Royal Mint to be coined. This time the name LIMA was inscribed below the portrait of King George II on coins minted in 1745 and 1746 (*Figure 25*). The choice of the name is puzzling, as although Lima is the capital of Peru, it is an inland city. The probability is that the name was conveniently short and fitted the space available in the coin design.

During the second half of the 18th century the Industrial Revolution brought a rapid increase in trade. People flocked to the

25 George II silver crown showing the name LIMA

large industrial towns to work in the new textile mills, coal-mines and factories. Farm-workers often took part of their wages in foodstuffs such as flour, vegetables or meat, but factory-owners needed money to pay their workers in cash. Small change was needed, too, by shop-keepers and tradesmen. Yet very few silver coins and even fewer copper coins were being produced by the Royal Mint. Between 1755 and 1769 and again between 1776 and 1798 no halfpennies or farthings were minted.

In desperation many factory-owners and tradesmen began to issue copper coins of their own. These private issues, known as tokens, are described in Chapter 10. Finally the government decided to grant a contract to the celebrated Birmingham engineer Matthew Boulton to produce copper pennies and twopenny pieces.

Matthew Boulton, with his Scottish partner James Watt, had installed steam-powered presses in his new factory at Soho, near Birmingham. He was able to produce all kinds of small metal trinkets, buttons, buckles, lamp fittings and similar items, very quickly and cheaply. The copper coins he minted in 1797 are among the most impressive coins ever used in Britain. Their obverse had a portrait of King George III (1760-1820) wearing a laurel wreath, the symbol of victory, and a Roman toga. On the reverse was a fine picture of Britannia with a trident in one hand and an olive branch, symbolising peace, in the other (*Figures 26, 27*).

The penny contained one pennyworth of copper and weighed one ounce. The twopenny piece contained twopence worth of copper, weighed two ounces and measured over 1½ ins (41 mms) in diameter. Known, for obvious reasons, as 'cartwheels', Matthew

26 Britannia on reverse of
George III penny, 1806

27 Britannia on reverse of
Queen Victoria penny, 1895

Boulton's coins proved too large and heavy to be convenient. The twopenny pieces were never re-issued but between 1799 and 1807 he minted smaller pennies, halfpennies and farthings in a similar design. These gradually replaced the unofficial tradesmen's tokens. So many of Matthew Boulton's handsome copper coins were issued that they are still quite common unless in perfect 'mint' condition. Worn examples are sometimes mistaken for Roman coins, because King George III was portrayed as if he had been a Roman emperor, but his name, GEORGIUS III, and the date are usually legible enough to identify the coins as British.

Before the long reign of King George III ended in 1820, another radical change was made in the British coinage. The Royal Mint was moved from the Tower of London to a new site on Tower Hill. Steam-powered machinery made by Boulton and Watt replaced the old hand-operated presses. At last the Royal Mint was capable of producing sufficient coins for the country's needs. In 1817 the old guineas and half-guineas were replaced by new gold coins, the sovereign and half-sovereign. The value of the sovereign was fixed at twenty shillings and a new design, showing St. George slaying the Dragon, was used for the reverse. This design can still be seen on sovereigns being minted for Queen Elizabeth II.

The reign of Queen Victoria (1837-1901) brought more changes. In a half-hearted attempt to introduce a decimal coinage, the Royal Mint issued silver florins, ten of which were worth one pound. The coins proved useful and popular but when, during the 1850s and 1860s, the Mint ceased making half-crowns, people complained until these were re-issued as well as the florins. The next step in decimalisation came in 1887, when large silver double-florins, or four-shilling pieces, were introduced (*Figure 28*). This time there were complaints that the new coins were too close in size and weight to the silver crowns, or five-shilling pieces. In a busy shop an assistant might easily take a double-florin to be a crown and give too much change to the customer. After being minted for four years, the double-florins were never re-issued and the scheme for gradual decimalisation was abandoned.

A more sensible change in 1860 was to replace the old copper coins, which were inconveniently large and heavy, by coins made of bronze. This is an alloy of copper with a little tin and zinc, making the coins more hard-wearing. The bronze coins were also smaller

28 Victoria silver double florin

29 'Bun' coins showing young Victoria

30 'Veiled head' portrait of Victoria on coin minted after 1893

and lighter. They are generally known as 'bun coins' because in the portrait used for them Queen Victoria is shown with her hair gathered in a 'bun' at the back of her head (*Figure 29*). In 1893 another portrait was introduced. Known to collectors as the Veiled Head, this showed the Queen as an old lady, with a veil hanging from the back of her head and over her shoulders (*Figure 30*).

A remarkable feature of Queen Victoria's coinage was the wide range of coins which circulated during her reign. At one time or other Victorians might have the following coins in their pockets:

Gold

£5 piece	£2 piece
sovereign	half-sovereign

Silver

crown	double-florin
half-crown	florin
shilling	sixpence
groat (4d)	threepence

Copper and Bronze

penny	halfpenny
farthing	half-farthing

This list does not include the silver Maundy coins, which were also legal tender (see Chapter 11).

The coins of King Edward VII (1901-1910) and King George V (1910-1936) followed a similar pattern to those of Queen Victoria. In order to save part of the cost of minting silver coins, the proportion of silver in them was reduced in 1920 from 92½% to only 50%. An even more drastic revision came during the reign of King George VI (1936-1952). Because Britain had borrowed heavily from the United States during the Second World War (1939-1945), silver was needed to repay the debt. After 1946, in order to save the precious metal, the 'silver' coins were made entirely of cupro-nickel, an alloy of copper and nickel. Only the little Maundy coins were exempted from this change.

Mention must be made of the coinage of King Edward VIII (1936). During the 1930s people, such as tram and bus conductors, who had to handle large amounts of small change, often complained that even the bronze halfpennies and pennies were too heavy for convenience. On the other hand they disliked the tiny silver threepenny pieces because these were so easily lost. To solve this problem the Royal Mint decided to introduce a new threepenny coin. Made of nickel and brass, this was dodecagonal, or twelve-sided, and weighed less than a quarter of the weight of three separate bronze pennies.

King Edward VIII succeeded to the throne in January 1936 and the Royal Mint at once began preparing coins bearing his portrait, among them the new brass threepences. The coins were almost ready for issue when the King abdicated in December 1936. A few of the brass threepences had been lent for testing purposes to firms making automatic vending machines, or slot machines, and a very small number of these coins, probably about a dozen, escaped into circulation. They are now very rare and valuable. The remainder of the Edward VIII coins, except for specimens kept by the Royal Mint, were melted down so that the metal in them could be used again (*Figure 31*).

The reign of King George VI brought other changes. Despite a few complaints at their unconventional appearance, the brass threepences proved useful and popular, so that after 1944 no more of the little silver threepenny pieces were minted for circulation (*Figure 32*). As a compliment to Queen Elizabeth, later the Queen Mother, who was of Scottish birth, a new design was used for the reverse of some of the shillings. This showed a Scottish-style lion, a thistle and St. Andrew's saltire, or cross. English-style shillings, with the lion standing on a large crown, were also issued and both

31 One of the coins minted for Edward VIII and not issued because of his abdication in 1936

32 George VI threepenny piece

coins could be used in either country. Some still survive as 5p coins but they are gradually being withdrawn from circulation.

During the reign of Queen Elizabeth II the most important change in the coinage has been the introduction of the decimal currency in 1971 (*Figure 33 see p. 40*). Other changes have included the disappearance of the farthing, which was not minted after 1956 because it had ceased to be useful, and the issue of the first coins since those of Oliver Cromwell to portray a person who was not a member of the Royal family, assuming that Britannia and St. George are regarded as legendary figures. In 1965, as a tribute to Sir Winston Churchill, who had died the previous year, cupro-nickel crowns with his portrait on one side and that of the Queen on the other were placed in circulation. Although many were saved as souvenirs, the Churchill crowns were seldom used for ordinary buying and selling, probably because they were too large for modern pockets and purses (*Figure 34*).

Also minted, but not for circulation, were the gold sovereigns. These had been withdrawn during the First World War (1914-1918) and replaced by paper money. A small number of George V sovereigns and half-sovereigns had been minted after the war but

34 Churchill crown minted after his death

33 Pre-decimal currency of Elizabeth II's reign

for King George VI they were minted only in 1937, his Coronation year. Most were bought by collectors. During the reign of Queen Elizabeth II sovereigns have again been minted because the Bank of England sometimes needs them for overseas transactions. They may also be bought by coin collectors who can afford them.

Since decimalisation special 25p coins, still known as crowns, have been issued to commemorate the Queen's silver wedding anniversary in 1972 and the silver jubilee of her accession. Britain's entry into the European Economic Community was commemorated in 1973 by the issue of special 50p coins. Instead of Britannia, these had nine clasped hands on the reverse, one for each member of the Community.

3
Making
a Start

One of the advantages of collecting coins as a hobby is that it needs no expensive equipment. While the collection is small, the coins can be kept in one of the shallow cardboard boxes in which shirts or writing-paper are sold. By pasting narrow strips of cardboard from end to end and from side to side of the box, the collector can make rows of small compartments in which the coins can be laid singly, so that they do not rub against one another. One or two such boxes will provide a temporary home until the collection has grown large enough to require more elaborate housing (see Chapter 6).

Apart from a temporary home for the collection, the first essential is a good magnifying-glass. This will reveal all kinds of details in the design of a coin that are not easily seen with the naked eye. A typical example occurs on the first pennies minted for King Edward VII in 1902. The picture of Britannia on the reverse of these coins was the same as that used on the last coins of Queen Victoria, dated 1901. At the right of the picture the line marking the horizon of the sea touches Britannia's right leg just below the point where this leg meets the front of her left leg. The distance from the base line of the picture, just above the date, to the horizon is 4·15 mms.

Later in 1902 the Royal Mint began to use a slightly different picture of Britannia on the reverse of the pennies. One difference, difficult to measure, is that the letter P of the word PENNY is a little closer to the top of Britannia's trident. A more important difference, which can be seen with a magnifying-glass, is that the sea horizon is a little higher. It meets Britannia's legs practically at the point where her legs cross. This point measures 4·4 mms from the base line. The early coins are known to collectors as the Low Tide pennies and the later coins as the High Tide pennies. The same difference can be seen on the 1902 halfpennies, and all the later pennies and halfpennies of Edward VII have the same High Tide. The difference is important because it affects the value of the coins from the collector's point of view. Because fewer were minted, the Low Tide pennies are worth three or four times as much as the High Tide pennies, while the Low Tide halfpennies are even more valuable, costing about ten times as much as those with the High Tide.

One of the first decisions the collector has to make is whether or not to clean and polish the coins he acquires. Even experienced collectors admit that there is a great temptation, when faced with a dull and grimy old bronze or copper coin, to dab it with metal polish and rub it briskly with a cloth until it shines. This is a temptation that should be resisted at all costs.

Bronze and copper coins are very prone to become corroded, especially in damp conditions. The corrosion takes the form of patches of verdigris, a green, powdery deposit that eats away the surface of the metal. Even if the verdigris is removed, the surface of the coin remains pitted and unsightly. Fortunately bronze and copper may acquire instead an even coating which is caused by a chemical reaction between the metal and the atmosphere. Known as a patina, this coating is usually green or dark brown and as it preserves the coin from corrosion, it should never be removed. Metal polish will destroy the patina, leaving the coin open to corrosion by verdigris.

An attractively coloured and even patina adds considerably to the value of an old coin. When an auctioneer is offering coins for sale he is always glad to mention in the sale catalogue any that have a particularly attractive patina. 'In very fine condition and has a dark green patina' is a typical catalogue description. If, on the other hand, a coin has been cleaned, this has to be mentioned regretfully: 'In very fine condition but has been cleaned'.

Bronze or copper coins that are very soiled, then, should be washed with soap in warm water and carefully dried on a soft cloth. Any spots of verdigris or obstinate specks of dirt should be picked out with a sharpened matchstick or a toothpick but never with a pin or a metal point, as this is likely to scratch the coin.

Silver coins do not normally corrode but they do become tarnished if they are kept in damp conditions or exposed to salt sea air. The modern 'silver dip' is safe to use on tarnished coins, which can then be washed and dried on a soft cloth. Although they do not have a patina, old silver coins sometimes take on a faint bluish or greenish tinge known as 'tone'. This, like the patina on an old bronze or copper coin, is considered by experienced collectors to be an added attraction, so it should not be removed. Washing in warm, not hot, water and careful drying should be sufficient to make a toned silver coin clean enough for a collection.

Gold coins are the most attractive for the collector who likes bright, clean specimens. Even after centuries buried in the earth, gold coins do not tarnish or corrode. A wash in warm, soapy water and gentle drying will soon restore a gold coin to its normal shining brightness. But both silver and gold are soft metals and can easily be scratched, especially by the stiff bristles of a brush, so careful handling is essential.

Even simply holding a coin in one's fingers may damage it. This is because a person's skin is never completely dry. The moisture on it is sufficient to stain the bright surface of a new silver or cupro-nickel coin, leaving a finger-print plain enough to delight the eye of a detective but unsightly to the coin collector. To avoid spoiling the appearance of a coin in this way, experienced collectors always hold it with thumb and fore-finger at the edge, taking care not to touch the flat surface on either side.

With these thoughts in mind, let us make a start by taking a few ordinary British coins from our pocket or purse to see what we can discover about them. Whatever their face value, they are likely to have one thing in common: they almost all have a portrait of the Queen on the obverse. This portrait was drawn by a Staffordshire-born artist, Arnold Machin, R.A. The same portrait was used on the new decimal coins issued in Australia in 1966 and in New Zealand the following year. It can also be seen on coins from many other Commonwealth countries, among them Canada, Mauritius, the Channel Islands and Hong Kong.

Round the portrait the British coins have an inscription in Latin abbreviations: ELIZABETH II D.G. REG. F.D., and the date. In full the Latin words would be: Elizabeth II, Dei Gratia Regina, Fidei Defensor (*Figure 35*). Latin is used because when inscriptions were first placed on British coins, more than a thousand years ago, this was the language used by educated people in the countries of western Europe where Roman influence had been strong. Even during the 8th century AD, King Offa had used the Latin form of

35 Latin inscription on pre-decimal penny

his title, OFFA REX, on his silver pennies.

The words DEI GRATIA REGINA mean 'By the Grace of God, Queen'. The title FIDEI DEFENSOR gives a false impression. It means 'Defender of the Faith' and it was conferred by the Pope on King Henry VIII in gratitude for a book the King had written attacking the new Protestant doctrines and defending the Roman Catholic Church. Later the King quarrelled with the Pope and declared himself to be the head of the Church in England but he retained the honorary title he had been given and it has been used by British monarchs ever since.

The reverse designs for the British decimal coins were the work of Christopher Ironside, who was a teacher at Maidstone College of Art, in Kent. At first glance the designs appear to be completely new. They certainly differ from those of the pre-decimal coins of Queen Elizabeth II, except that Britannia, who used to be depicted on the pre-decimal penny, was transferred to the decimal 50p coin. The long history of Britannia has already been mentioned but some of the other decimal designs have almost equally historic origins. The numeral with the crown above it, on the ½p coin, continues a tradition which began during the reign of King James II (1685-1688). His smaller silver 1d, 2d, 3d, and 4d coins had the Latin numeral with a crown above it on the reverse and a similar design has been used ever since then for the little silver Maundy coins.

The portcullis on the 1p coin has an even longer history, for King Henry VII (1485-1509) used a portcullis as one of his badges and it formed part of the reverse design of rare silver groats minted during the early years of his reign. In modern times a portcullis has been featured on the pre-decimal brass threepences of Queen Elizabeth II.

The three ostrich plumes, popularly known as the Prince of Wales's feathers because they are his traditional badge, may be found on several silver coins minted for King Charles I during the Civil War. Tiny pennies made in the temporary mint at Aberystwyth about 1640 have a reverse design very similar to the 2p coins of 1971.

The thistle on the reverse of the cupro-nickel 5p coins is the badge of Scotland. It was used on many Scottish coins minted for the Stuart kings and on the bawbee, or Scottish sixpence, of King Charles II there was a crown above the thistle, just as there is on the 5p coins. The design of the 10p coins, however, is new. Although lions have often appeared in the designs of British coins, none have been as lively as Christopher Ironside's vigorous animal.

It is possible that the coins in our pocket or purse may include one or two of the pre-decimal shillings and florins which are still in circulation as 5p and 10p coins respectively. If so, these may have a portrait of King George V or King George VI and two additional Latin titles, abbreviated as BR. OMN. REX or BRITT. OMN. REX, and IND. IMP. The first stands for BRITANNIARUM OMNIUM REX and means 'King of all the Britains', showing that the monarch was the ruler of all the British countries overseas as well as of Great Britain itself. This title was also used on the first coins of Queen Elizabeth II but as more Commonwealth countries have become independent, the title has been omitted from coins minted after 1953.

The abbreviation IND. IMP., standing for INDIAE IMPERATRIX or INDIAE IMPERATOR, means Empress, or Emperor, of India. Queen Victoria was proclaimed Empress of India in 1877 and the title first appeared on her coins in 1893. Her successors used the title as Emperor of India and it was inscribed on their coins, but India became independent in 1947 and King George VI then gave up the title. After 1948 it disappeared from his coins.

If, among the decimal coins, there is one of the two-shilling pieces, or florins, of Queen Elizabeth II, the design of the reverse is well worth studying with a magnifying-glass. In the centre, representing England, is a Tudor rose, so called because it was one of the badges of the first Tudor monarch, King Henry VII.

Arranged to form a pattern round the rose are the floral emblems of the other parts of the United Kingdom, thistles for Scotland, leeks for Wales and shamrock for Northern Ireland. Just above the two letters I in the word SHILLINGS can be seen the initials of the artists who designed the reverse of the coin, Edgar Fuller and Cecil Thomas.

4
Pictures
in our Pockets

So many coins have been minted during the last two thousand years that forming a general collection of world issues would be a formidable task. Even to collect one specimen from each country where coins have been issued during the 20th century would require a great deal of time and money. Crete, Danzig, Estonia, Saxony and Montenegro are only a few of the many states which ceased to have their own coinage when they were absorbed into larger countries. Some of these obsolete coins are now scarce and expensive.

a) penny (*obverse*)

b) half penny (*obverse*)

c) three penny piece (*obverse*)

a) penny (*reverse*)

b) half penny (*reverse*)

c) three penny piece (*reverse*)

36 Guernsey coinage

As a result most collectors concentrate on the coins of a single country or group of countries. Those of Great Britain, the Channel Islands (*Figure 36*), Canada, Australia and New Zealand are particularly popular but coins from Scandinavia, India, the United States and the smaller British Commonwealth countries are also widely collected. Collectors of British coins usually specialise still further by concentrating on one or two denominations. Farthings, pennies, shillings and halfcrowns seem to be the favourites but the large silver crowns are handsome coins for those who can afford them.

In recent years a new kind of collecting, known as thematic or topical collecting, has become popular. This means choosing a single theme or topic and collecting the coins which illustrate it, regardless of the countries from which they come. Portraits of queens and other women rulers, coats-of-arms, wild birds, flowers, ships and musical instruments can all form interesting topics for a collection. The most popular choice is probably the Coin Zoo (*Figures 37, 38, 39*).

a) United States
quarter - eagle

b) Great Britain
farthing - wren

c) United States
half dollar - eagle

d) Ireland one penny
- hen & chicks

e) Germany two
marks - eagle

37 Coins showing birds

a) Germany 10 pfennig

b) Italy 100 lira

c) Great Britain 6p

d) France 1 franc

e) France 5 francs

f) Denmark 25 ore

38 Coins showing plants

a) Australian penny - kangaroo

b) Canada 50 cents - wolf

c) South Africa five shillings springbok

d) Ireland half crown - race horse

39 Coins showing animals

Because the lion is regarded as a symbol of strength and courage, many countries have issued coins with lions in their designs. The shillings issued between 1902 and 1951 provide examples of the British lion, though the lions in a real zoo are unlikely to be wearing a crown. The lion is also the emblem of Belgium, Finland, Czechoslovakia and Iran, so examples can be found on many coins from those countries. In West Africa the Gambia provides an attractive 8-shillings coin with a picture of a hippopotamus and South Africa has issued several coins depicting its national animal, the springbok. Australia offers a kangaroo, the United States a bison (usually misnamed a buffalo), and Cyprus the wild mountain sheep known as the mouflon.

If the collector prefers domestic animals, the coins of Ireland provide some fine examples. Until 1928 ordinary British coins were used throughout Ireland but in that year the Irish Free State issued its first coinage. Designed by a Yorkshire sculptor, Percy Metcalfe, the eight coins in the series each depicted a different Irish animal, bird or fish. The halfpenny showed a sow with her piglets, the threepence a hare and the sixpence an Irish wolfhound. On the shilling was a stalwart bull and on the halfcrown a slender racehorse. These designs, with a woodcock, a hen and chickens, and a salmon on the other coins, were so popular that they attracted many collectors and gave Ireland useful publicity. When the new Irish decimal coins were being designed for issue in 1971, the bull, the salmon and the woodcock were retained on the new 5p, 10p and 50p coins respectively. It is only to be expected that an Isle of Man coin has a picture of a Manx cat, while a Guernsey coin depicts a cow and a Gibraltar 25p coin shows one of the celebrated apes which inhabit the upper slopes of the Rock. Even if they are not strictly domestic animals, the apes are tame and mischievous enough to be popular with everyone who visits Gibraltar.

An interesting and attractive collection can be formed of coins with the different portraits of Queen Elizabeth II (*Figure 40*). The first British coins of her reign, dated 1953, showed the Queen wearing a laurel wreath tied at the back with a gently fluttering ribbon. Designed by a Nottingham artist, Mrs. Mary Gillick, the same portrait was used on the coins of many Commonwealth countries, among them Australia, Canada and New Zealand. To commemorate the Queen's Coronation in 1953 the Royal Mint

a) Laurel wreath & ribbon,
pre-decimal currency.

b) Coronation crown

c) Silver Jubilee crown

d) Tiara - Isle of Man jubilee crown

e) Imperial State Crown-British Caribbean
Territories 25c

40 Coins showing portraits of Elizabeth II

issued special five-shilling pieces, or crowns. On these the Queen
was portrayed riding side-saddle on horseback and wearing the
uniform of Colonel-in-Chief of the Grenadier Guards. This
unusual design was the work of Gilbert Ledward, R.A.

For the British decimal coins the Royal Mint used a portrait by Arnold Machin, R.A., showing the Queen wearing a diamond tiara which was given to her as a wedding present by her grandmother, the late Queen Mary. This portrait had already been used on the new decimal coins of Australia and New Zealand, and on Canadian coins first issued in 1965.

To mark the Queen's Silver Jubilee, the 25th anniversary of her accession to the throne, the Royal Mint issued 25p commemorative coins in the crown size. The obverse of these showed the Queen on horseback in a pose similar to that on the 1953 crowns, but with minor differences in the set of the horse's head and the position of its legs.

In addition to these four portraits of Queen Elizabeth II on British coins, others can be found on coins from Commonwealth countries. Bermuda, Mauritius and Nigeria are among those which have used on their coins a dignified portrait of the Queen wearing the Imperial State Crown.

For the collector whose is interested in heraldry, an attractive display can be made of coins which have a coat-of-arms in their design. A study of these coins may reveal a great deal of a country's history. The coat-of-arms of the English monarchs dates from the reign of King Richard I (1189-1199), known as Richard the Lionheart. Very appropriately he chose three lions as his device. They were painted in gold on a red shield.

The moneyers who minted coins for King Richard and his successors were not skilled enough to include the coat-of-arms in the designs. Not until the 14th century were the royal arms seen on coins. In 1328 the King of France died without leaving a male heir. The English King Edward III claimed the throne because his mother had been a French princess. The French nobles preferred a local claimant, Philip of Valois. Edward III then asserted his claim by invading France, starting a conflict which was to last for more than a century, the Hundred Years' War. When new gold coins were minted in 1351 they showed the King holding a shield on which were the three lions of England and the fleur-de-lis of France.

For more than two hundred years the English royal coat-of-arms consisted of a shield divided into four parts, or quartered, as this arrangement is known in heraldry. In two quarters the shield had the three lions and in the other two the fleur-de-lis. When King James VI of Scotland succeeded Queen Elizabeth I as King of England, the royal arms had to be changed. The rampant lion of Scotland was placed in one quarter and the Irish harp in another, leaving two quarters for the English lions and the French fleurs-de-lis. This splendid coat-of-arms can be seen on many gold and silver coins of King James I and the later Stuart monarchs.

When Queen Anne, the last Stuart ruler, died in 1714 she was succeeded by a German relative, George of Hanover. His coat-of-arms, whose main feature was a silver horse, had to be added to the old royal arms of Great Britain. This was done by placing the English lions and the Scottish rampant lion in the same quarter, leaving the vacant quarter to be occupied by the arms of Hanover. Many gold and silver coins of the first three Georges show this new coat-of-arms. The Latin inscriptions on their coins also showed that the kings claimed to be 'By the Grace of God, King of Great Britain, France and Ireland, Defender of the Faith, Duke of Brunswick and Luneberg, Arch-Treasurer and Elector of the Holy Roman Empire'.

The use of these high-sounding but empty titles came to an end after 1802. By that time France had become a republic with a new ruler, Napoleon Bonaparte. After almost ten years of war, Britain and France made a temporary peace in a treaty signed at Amiens. One of the terms of this treaty was that the King of Great Britain should cease to claim that he was also the King of France. The French fleur-de-lis then disappeared from the royal coat-of-arms. The later coins minted for King George III and those of his successors, King George IV (1820-1830) and King William IV (1830-1837) show the coat-of-arms with the English lions again occupying two of the four quarters in the shield.

The Hanoverian coat-of-arms was now superimposed in the centre of the shield but it disappeared after the accession of Queen Victoria in 1837. As a woman she was not allowed to reign in Hanover, where all the monarchs were male. Hanover then ceased to be part of the British dominions and the royal coat-of-arms assumed the form it still has today. The first and fourth quarters show the three lions of England, the second quarter shows the Scottish lion and the third quarter shows the Irish harp. This coat-of-arms can be seen on many British coins minted since 1837. The

a) Malagasy Republic

b) Uganda

c) Somali Republic

d) Rwanda

41 FAO coins

halfcrowns are particularly attractive because the designers in each reign have used different shapes for the shield on which the coat-of-arms is displayed.

Many other countries have issued coins featuring their coats-of-arms. That of Australia can be seen on florins first minted in 1953 and on 50-cents coins of 1966. Several Canadian coins show Canada's coat-of-arms and the New Zealand coat-of-arms appears on the handsome dollars minted since 1967. The Bahamas, the Cayman Islands, Mauritius and Sierra Leone are among the other British Commonwealth countries which can be included in a collection of 'coats-of-arms on coins', and dozens of foreign countries provide other examples. Kindred collections may also be made of coins featuring national flags, floral emblems, and the birds and animals chosen by different countries as their national symbols. The American eagle, the French cock, the Japanese chrysanthemum and the cedar of Lebanon are among the national badges familiar to coin collectors.

Occasionaly coins are minted for a special campaign. In 1968 the Food and Agriculture Organisation of the United Nations launched a campaign to persuade people to grow more food. As part of the campaign the F.A.O. invited member countries to issue special coins with such slogans as 'Grow More Food' and 'Food for All'. These are some of the coins which have been minted to support the F.A.O. campaign (*Figure 41*).

5
Building
a Collection

Having examined the contents of his or her pocket or purse, the coin collector is then faced with the problem of how to build an interesting and attractive collection. Because they are so easy to obtain, it is sensible to start with the ordinary decimal coins. The change from the old £ s d coinage to the decimal currency was officially made on 15 February 1971 but even before that date three of the new decimal coins were already in circulation in Britain. They were the 5p, 10p and 50p coins.

Because the new 5p and 10p coins were to be in the same size as the old shillings and florins they were intended to replace, the Royal Mint was able to start producing them in 1968, so that is the earliest date for them. The next decimal coin to appear was the seven-sided 50p, which was intended to replace the old ten-shilling Bank of England note. The first of the 50p coins were dated 1969. By keeping a careful eye on the decimal coins he receives in his change, the collector can eventually assemble a complete series, with an example dated each year that the various coins were minted.

The next step in building a collection is to ask one's family and friends if they have any old coins which they no longer want. People who spend holidays abroad or have to travel overseas on business frequently return home with a few coins which they cannot exchange at the bank. Many of these coins may be badly worn or damaged from having been in circulation but occasionally travellers return with small change in practically mint condition, entirely suitable for a collection. It might be a good idea for the collector to mention to members of the family or friends going abroad that he would welcome a few new coins as souvenirs.

Coins collected in this way are likely to be modern issues and the collector seeking older and more valuable coins must look elsewhere for them. One obvious method is to exchange with other collectors. Unfortunately exchanging coins by post, especially with people in other countries, is sometimes difficult because of postal or customs regulations. Strictly speaking coins should be sent only by registered mail, which is expensive, although a single coin securely packed between pieces of cardboard may usually pass through the post without comment from the post office. But if it is lost in these circumstances, the collector would not be entitled to compensation.

More satisfactory exchanges can be made by becoming a member of the local coin collectors' club. Almost all large towns have at least one numismatic society and older members will be glad to welcome a young collector or an adult beginner to their meetings. These are usually held once a month, or fortnightly if the members are enthusiastic enough. The meeting-place may be in a room at the local public library, a schoolroom or, in the case of the smaller societies, at the home of each member in turn.

The programme normally includes lectures by visiting experts, who bring specimens or slides to illustrate their subject, and informal displays or talks by the society members themselves. Time is always allowed for friendly discussion and exchanges, and most societies have a small library of useful handbooks and catalogues which members may borrow.

The local library will provide the name and address of the honorary secretaries of the nearest numismatic societies. The answer for the collector who lives too far from any of the societies is simply to enlist the help of a few like-minded friends and to start a club himself. Collectors still at school may find a member of staff willing to help with the formation of a coin club. The teachers of history and geography are perhaps the most likely to be interested in coins, since these illustrate so many of the topics they teach.

Eventually the collector will wish to buy coins from a dealer. The easiest way to make contact with dealers is to read the advertisements in one of the numismatic magazines. In these the dealers list the coins they are offering for sale, the condition of each coin and its price. Unlike stamp dealers, who will send selections of cheap stamps on approval, coin dealers expect payment to be sent in advance, except from collectors whom they know personally. On the other hand, almost all coin dealers will refund the money paid for the coins if the collector returns these within a short time, usually seven or ten days, provided that the coins have not been damaged in any way.

These conditions are plainly stated in the advertisements. Other points to look for include the amount required for postage and whether any discount is offered on purchases totalling more than a certain amount. Many dealers issue price-lists or catalogues of the coins they have in stock. These are very useful to the collector because they show the current retail prices of the coins he is seeking. By comparing the prices charged by different dealers, he may sometimes find a bargain.

In recent years an increasing number of trade fairs have been held in different parts of the country. Dealers in coins, banknotes, stamps, picture postcards and similar items lay out their stocks on trestle tables in a large room at the local hotel, in a school or church hall. The organisers charge a small admission fee, about 10p for young collectors and 25p for adults, and anyone who wishes can then browse among the items on display, buying any he wants at the prices marked on them. Most coin dealers have boxes of mixed coins at a standard price, perhaps 10p or 20p each, as well as trays of better specimens at higher prices. The main disadvantage of these fairs is that there is usually a jostling crowd round each table but anyone who likes hunting for bargains and has a sharp pair of elbows may spend an enjoyable hour or two.

Several of the larger firms of coin dealers run auction sales which collectors can attend in person or to which they can send bids by post. The sales catalogues resemble dealers' price-lists except that the prices quoted for each lot are only the auctioneer's estimate of its value. If several bidders all wish to buy the same lot, they may bid against one another until the lot is sold to the highest bidder at well above the original estimate.

The sales catalogues also contain a printed form on which collectors may make a list of their bids for various lots if they cannot attend the sale in person. Knowing how much to bid for a coin without seeing it requires a good deal of experience and faith in the honesty of the auctioneer's description of it in the catalogue. Auctioneers do not normally accept bids from anyone under eighteen years of age, so younger collectors wishing to bid at auction need the advice and sponsorship of an adult.

Whether exchanging coins or buying them from dealers or at auction, the collector must above all pay close attention to their condition. In deciding the value of a coin this is the most important consideration. Other factors, such as its age or date, its scarcity, the metal of which it is made, and the artistic quality of its design, may all affect the value of a coin, but its condition is more important than any of these.

As an example, dealers normally charge about £5 for a specimen of the copper twopenny piece minted by Matthew Boulton in 1797, if it is in 'fine' condition. The same coin costs £15 if in 'very fine' condition and £70 or £75 if it is 'extremely fine'. For a specimen in 'mint' condition, meaning that it has never been in circulation, the price would be in the region of £150 to £200.

In deciding the condition of a coin, dealers and collectors use the following terms, usually in their abbreviated form:

Poor, abbreviated as **P**
Mediocre *or* **M**
Very Good *or* **VG**
Fair *or* **Fr**
Fine *or* **F**
Very Fine *or* **VF**
Extremely Fine *or* **EF**
Uncirculated *or* **Unc**
Fleur de coin *or* **FDC**
Proof

Poor The coin is damaged, corroded or so badly worn that the inscriptions and date are illegible. A coin in this condition would interest a collector only if it were exceptionally rare and unobtainable in any other condition.

Mediocre A little better than a Poor specimen but not much! Ordinary coins in this condition would not be of interest to a collector but a very rare coin might be acceptable if nothing better is available.

Very Good This is a misleading term, because a Very Good coin is in fact a very bad specimen, showing plain signs of wear, damage or corrosion. But the main features of the design are identifiable and the date and inscriptions are legible.

Fair Still a low grade of condition and acceptable only if a better specimen would cost more than the collector can afford. The main features of the design are worn flat but are legible and there may also be slight damage or corrosion.

Fine A coin in Fine condition shows obvious signs of having been in circulation for a considerable time. The most prominent parts of the design are worn flat, so that details such as the lines of the hair in the portrait, or the faces of lions or other animals in a coat-of-arms, have almost disappeared. Although it is clearly worn, a coin in Fine condition is acceptable even to a fastidious collector if better specimens are too expensive.

Very Fine A coin in this condition shows signs of having been in circulation for a short time. Some details of the design may have been lost but the general appearance is sharp and distinct. This is an acceptable condition for almost all coins except modern issues which are plentiful in even better condition.

Extremely Fine In this condition a coin has only very slight traces of wear at a few places in the most prominent parts of the design. This wear may have been caused by the coin having been in circulation for a very brief period or even by being carelessly handled by a collector. For all coins except the most modern issues, Extremely Fine is a perfectly acceptable grade of condition. It is the normal condition of coins that are more than about fifty or sixty years old.

Uncirculated As the name indicates, an Uncirculated coin is one that has never been in normal circulation. It has probably passed direct from the Royal Mint to a bank and thence to a collector. The coin would show no signs of wear except that because modern coins are transported in bags, there may be slight abrasions or scuff marks where it has been in contact with other coins. The term 'Mint State' is sometimes used to signify Uncirculated. Some dealers also add the prefix 'Brilliant', usually abbreviated to **B. Unc.** or **B.U.**

Fleur de coin This term is a French expression meaning 'the flower of the coin'. It was used by collectors many years ago to describe a coin in perfect mint state, with no flaw of any kind. Because of the mechanical handling to which they are subjected at the Royal Mint, it is not possible to obtain modern coins in **FDC** condition unless they are Proof specimens.

Proof A Proof coin can be recognised by its bright, mirror-like surface. It has been minted from specially polished dies which produce a sharp, clear design, and it has been carefully handled throughout the minting process at the Royal Mint, so that it has not even the slightest blemish. Proof coins are intended for sale to collectors and are usually sold in neat boxes or plastic containers. Because they are much more expensive to buy from the Royal Mint than coins intended for ordinary use, Proof coins are found in circulation only by accident.

Although these ten grades of condition are recognised as the standard guide, dealers often add their own terms to describe individual coins. Thus a **GF** coin is one in Good Fine condition, meaning that its condition lies between Fine and Very Fine. Near **EF** means that the coin is almost, but not quite, Extremely Fine. One description used by dealers, Near **Unc**, causes a great deal of controversy, as some collectors consider it illogical to claim that a coin has 'nearly not been in circulation'. Either the coin has been in circulation, they say, or it has not.

As well as its condition, there are several other factors which affect the value of a coin. The number minted, known as the mintage, is important because this determines the number available for collectors. In 1948, for example, 4,230,400 of the brass three-pences bearing the portrait of King George VI were minted. In 1949 the mintage was only 464,000. As a result the 1949 coin is almost ten times scarcer than the 1948 coin and this is reflected in their values. In uncirculated condition the 1948 brass threepence now costs about £10 but the 1949 coin in the same condition would cost about £90 or £100.

The metal of which a coin is made also affects its value. Gold and silver are precious metals, so that no matter what the condition of a gold or silver coin may be, it has an intrinsic value. But brass, copper and bronze are comparatively cheap metals, with almost no intrinsic value of their own. With experience the collector learns to balance these factors against one another, so that he can build an attractive collection of coins which are likely to increase in value as time goes by.

6
A Home for the Collection

The coin collector has a choice of several methods of housing his collection. Dealers with a large stock of coins usually keep them in coin envelopes. Made of brown manilla or white cartridge paper, these measure 2″ by 2″ (50 by 50 mms) with a flap on one side. Details of the coins they contain can be written on the outside of the envelopes and these can be stored upright in cardboard boxes specially made for the purpose. Index cards can be used to separate the coins of different countries or face values, so that any coin can be found at a moment's notice. This method of storage may be ideal for a busy dealer but for the collector it has the disadvantage that the coins have to be taken out of their envelopes if they are needed for study or to display to friends.

Too much handling may damage or tarnish the surface of new coins, so many collectors use instead envelopes of the same size but made of transparent vinyl. These envelopes can also be stored in boxes and the coins need not be taken out for display. To prevent small coins from slipping about inside the envelopes coin cards have recently been introduced. These are small pieces of thin white cardboard which fit closely into the envelopes. In the centre of each card there is a circular hole. When the coin is placed in this and the card is slipped into the vinyl envelope, the coin is held firmly in place. Cards with holes to fit different coins, from a farthing to a crown, can be bought from dealers at a penny or two each.

Collectors who prefer to house their coins in an album can buy loose-leaf binders containing vinyl pages with rows of pockets similar to the coin envelopes. The standard size of page has sixteen pockets and a loose-leaf binder will normally hold at least a dozen pages, so that the complete album will accomodate almost 200 coins. Coin cards can be used in the vinyl pockets and white cardboard can be used for interleaving the pages, providing the collector with space in which to write or print details of the coins on each page.

As the vinyl pages can be bought separately from the binders, some collectors store them instead in cardbox boxes. This enables the collection to be displayed and re-housed very easily and quickly.

For a small collection of valuable coins the collector may wish to buy a coin cabinet. This can be as large as a chest of drawers or as small as a chocolate-box. It contains flat wooden trays with circular recesses in which the coins are fitted. Below each coin the collector usually places a disc of black or dark green felt, known as a roundel. This protects the coin from scratches and also improves its appearance by providing a contrasting background. Below the felt roundel there is room for a small disc of white cardboard on which details of the coins can be written.

The trays should be made of a well-dried wood which has no resin or natural oils in it, as these may tarnish or discolour the coins. The best woods for the purpose are rosewood and mahogany but unfortunately these are expensive. It is now possible to buy coin trays made of hardboard or fibreboard. This may have a pungent odour and tends to tarnish silver and cupro-nickel coins over a period of several years, so regular airing of the collection is essential.

One disadvantage of arranging coins in trays is that normally all the recesses in a single tray are the same size. This is convenient for the collector who is making a collection of, for example, farthings, shillings or halfcrowns, because each type of coin can be arranged in the tray which has suitable recesses. But anyone collecting sets of coins running from a farthing to a crown is unlikely to be able to arrange the coins of different sizes in the same tray.

Wooden cabinets to hold as many as forty or fifty trays of coins can be bought from dealers but the cost of these puts them beyond the reach of most collectors. It is preferable to concentrate on forming a small collection of well chosen coins, so that only a few trays are needed to house it. These can be stored in a stout cardboard box or, if the collector has a talent for carpentry or can enlist the help of a cabinet-maker or carpenter, in a home-made wooden box.

The advantages of using trays for housing a collection are

obviously that the coins are attractively displayed, they can easily be studied and as the collection becomes larger more trays can be obtained to accomodate the new acquisitions.

Many countries now offer sets of their coins for sale to collectors. The sets usually contain one coin of each value and are arranged in neat plastic cases with a space for each coin. Because of the differing numbers of coins in the various sets, the cases are in different shapes and sizes. Individual coins are also sometimes sold in specially made boxes.

For coins not supplied in cases or boxes, collectors may now buy empty cases with a recess to hold the coin, a padded lid to protect it from damage and a attractive imitation leather cover. These cases resemble those in which jewellers sell rings and brooches but as they cost from about £1 each, they are suitable only for particularly choice or valuable coins. For ordinary coins the most suitable home is provided by the vinyl envelopes, the vinyl pages of coin albums or the hardboard coin trays.

7
How Coins
are Made

Knowing how coins have been made at various times in their long history may help the collector to identify unusual specimens and to understand how errors or varieties in their designs have occurred. It may also lead him to appreciate the skill of the moneyers of ancient Greece, for example, who were able to create artistic masterpieces while using only primitive tools.

The earliest coins were simply oval lumps of metal on which a simple design was punched by a craftsman striking an iron die with his hammer. When the Greeks began to make coins with a design on both sides, two dies had to be used, one for the obverse and the other for the reverse. The die for the obverse design was known as the pile, from a Latin word meaning a pillar. The die for the reverse design was the trussel, from a word meaning a bar.

The preparation of the dies was a task requiring skill and patience. They were made from thick pieces of cast iron about eight inches long and shaped like a modern stick of seaside rock. One end of the pile was filed smooth and the other tapered to a point. On the smooth end the craftsman had to carve or scratch with sharp tools the design of the obverse side of the coin. He carved the design back to front because it would then be the right way round on the finished coin. Even the lettering had to be back to front. When the pile was ready it was fixed by the point in a large block of wood.

From another length of cast iron bar the craftsman then carved the die for the reverse of the coin, the trussel. The opposite end of the trussel was left flat because the moneyer would have to hit this with his hammer. Meanwhile other workmen had cut discs from a flattened strip of the metal from which the coins were to be made. After being filed down to the required size and weight these blank discs were heated to make the metal more malleable. Using a pair of pincers a workman held a disc on the pile while the moneyer placed the trussel on top and gave it a sharp blow with his hammer. This impressed the design on both sides of the coin at once.

This method of minting coins was used in Europe for many centuries. In China, where the early coins were shaped like miniature knives, spades and other tools, they were cast by pouring the molten metal into moulds. The Romans improved on the ancient Greek method by fixing the two dies on to the arms of large pincers so that they registered exactly when brought together and hammered. Another Roman improvement was to sink the pile into an iron anvil, leaving a space at the top into which the blank disc of metal could be fitted. This held it firmly in place while the moneyer hammered the trussel. In a ruined house in Pompeii, the Roman city destroyed by an eruption of Mount Vesuvius in AD 79, there is a wall painting showing the various stages of production in a Roman mint.

Other improvements were made during Norman times in the cutting of the dies. The moneyers made a series of punches which they could use for building up the design. A favourite punch was one which made a tiny round dent in the die. This appeared on the finished coin as a small round lump, like a pellet. Almost every coin minted in England between the Norman Conquest of 1066 and the early 16th century has some of these pellets in its design. They were used as decorations, as jewels in the king's crown, to make the head of his sceptre, and even in many cases for his eyes.

The letters on Norman coins look as if they had been made with tiny sausages. This is because many of the letters were composed of two or more punches. A half-circle was used for the letter **C**. Turned round and struck alongside an **I** it would make the letter **D**. The letter **E** could be made by putting a tiny horizontal mark, like a hyphen -, in the centre of a **C**. The punch used for the letter I could also provide the king with his nose. All these tricks eased the craftsman's task of carving the dies but they also make the lettering on Norman and later coins very difficult to read.

In 1561 a French moneyer, Eloi Mestrelle, came from the Paris Mint to work at the Royal Mint in the Tower of London. He brought with him new machinery which made much neater and more regular blanks for making coins and also a screw-press for producing the coins themselves. The press was like a ship's capstan

42 Royal Mint. A metal copy of the artist's model of the new coinage effigy on the reducing machine. This is one of the first stages in making a die

or an old printing-press. Driven by a horse walking round and round, the press simply screwed down one die hard on to the blank disc of metal lying on the lower die in the anvil. Although the coins produced by this screw-press were of far better appearance than the old hammered coins, the new method was slower. When workmen at the Mint complained about the introduction of foreign machinery, Mestrelle was ordered to remove himself and his screw-press from the Tower. Unhappily he must have continued to use the press for some unofficial money-making, for in 1578 he was hanged at Tyburn for counterfeiting coins.

Almost fifty years later another Frenchman, Nicholas Briot, came from the Paris Mint, bringing new machinery for making coins. He was appointed as chief engraver at the Royal Mint and was also asked to supervise the work of the Scottish Mint in Edinburgh. Between 1631 and 1638 Briot produced some well-

43 Coins being minted

made gold and silver coins, using a metal collar which gripped the metal blanks as they were struck, so preventing them from spreading unevenly under the blow of the upper die. The collar also gave the milled edge, known as the graining, which finally put an end to the dishonest practice of clipping scraps of metal from a coin. Unfortunately the outbreak of the Civil War between King Charles I and his Parliament prevented Briot from continuing his work in the Royal Mint. He retired to Oxford, where the King had his headquarters, but died before the war was over.

The Restoration of King Charles II in 1660, and the need for a complete new series of coins bearing his portrait, brought the opportunity for yet more experiments with new machinery. This time it was another Frenchman, Pierre Blondeau, and a family of Dutch engravers, Philip Roettier and his three sons, who succeeded in persuading the Master of the Royal Mint to install machines for rolling the sheets of metal, cutting out the blanks, milling and engraving the edges and impressing the designs with the dies. The screw-press was worked by two men, with a boy removing the finished coin and replacing it by a blank. This process was quicker and more economical, as well as producing better quality coins, than any of the old methods. After 1662 hammered coins were no longer produced by the Royal Mint.

The next important change in coin-making came when Matthew Boulton won his contract to mint the large copper pennies and twopenny pieces in 1797. The increase in Britain's population and the rapid growth in trade following ·the Industrial Revolution brought a need for an up-to-date method of producing more coins than ever before. It was natural that Matthew Boulton's celebrated steam engines should provide the necessary power. At first the coins were produced in Boulton's factory at Soho, near Birmingham, but in 1810 he installed the steam-driven presses in a new Mint building on Tower Hill, London. The presses remained in constant use for about seventy years before being replaced by more modern machinery.

The most recent change in coin-making in Britain has been the transfer of the Royal Mint from Tower Hill to a new site at Llantrisant, in South Wales. The first part of the new building was opened in 1968 and the Queen, accompanied by the Duke of Edinburgh and the Prince of Wales, struck the first coins at Llantrisant on 17

December 1968. Coin production at Tower Hill ceased in November 1975, thus ending the long history of the London Mint. It is almost two thousand years since the first coins were minted in London by the Romans and about seven hundered years since the Royal Mint was installed in the Tower of London. Today's coining presses can each produce more coins in one minute than a Roman or Norman moneyer could make in a week (*Figures 42 & 43*).

Another British mint where coins have been made for over a hundred years is the Birmingham Mint. This is a private company founded in 1794 by Ralph Heaton, who specialised in making buttons, buckles and other small metal products. The company prospered when Heaton's five sons joined it and in 1850 they bought some of the coin-presses from Matthew Boulton's old factory at Soho. Using these, the company turned to minting coins, not only for Britain but for many countries overseas.

To identify the coins it made, the company included a tiny letter **H** in their designs. This mint-mark can be seen on Queen Victoria bun pennies dated 1874, 1875, 1876, 1881 and 1882. During the reign of King George V the company minted pennies in 1912, 1918 and 1919. Even after the company changed its name to the Birmingham Mint, it continued to use the **H** mint-mark. It is still a thriving company, making all kinds of metal items from coins and medallions to buttons and soldiers' badges.

Another Birmingham firm, the Kings Norton Metal Company, now part of Imperial Metal Industries, has also minted coins and medals for many years. Its mint-mark, the initials **KN**, can be seen on King George V pennies dated 1918 and 1919. In recent years the company has minted coins for Kenya, Uganda, Zambia and many other countries.

After gold was discovered in New South Wales in 1851, the Australian state governments were faced with the problem of transporting it on the long and hazardous journey to the Royal Mint in London, so that the precious metal could be minted into coins. Instead they decided to have it minted at the Assay Office in Adelaide, South Australia. A few years later a properly equipped mint was opened in Sydney and here, between 1855 and 1870, sovereigns and half-sovereigns bearing the name AUSTRALIA were minted. Other mints were then opened in Melbourne and Perth, and later in Ottawa, Canada, Bombay in India and Pretoria in South Africa. Gold coins were produced in all these mints in the same designs as those produced by the Royal Mint in London, but most issues had a mint-mark to identify them. The mint-marks were:

Sydney	S	Ottawa	C
Melbourne	M	Bombay	I
Perth	P	Pretoria	SA

These issues of British gold coins from overseas mints ceased in 1932.

8
Coins
of Many Kinds

Almost all British coins have been circular but occasionally there have been coins in other shapes. Some of the coins issued in besieged towns during the Civil War of the 1640s were diamond-shaped or octagonal. The dodecagonal brass threepences issued in 1937 have already been mentioned and when the decimal coinage was introduced in 1971, one of the new coins was the heptagonal, or seven-sided, 50p.

The earliest Chinese coins, shaped like miniature knives and spades, resembled children's toys but some of the early Japanese coins were dainty and artistic. They were large, thin, oval pieces of gold stamped with flower designs and with the value of each coin written on it in black ink. Later coins in both China and Japan were circular, with a large square hole in the centre. Many other countries have also issued coins with a hole through them. There are several reasons for this.

In tropical countries, where people wore only light clothing, perhaps without pockets, it was convenient to have a hole in the coins because these could be strung like a necklace on a piece of string. The hole also enabled coins to be distinguished easily from other coins of a similar size but without a hole. Finally and perhaps most important, by putting a hole in the coins, governments were able to issue coins of a convenient size while using much less metal than would have been needed for conventional coins without the hole.

A glance through a coin catalogue will show that some countries have issued coins in several different shapes. During the 1930s Egypt used coins with a hole in the centre, coins with a wavy or scalloped edge and octagonal coins. In 1944 new hexagonal, or six-sided, coins were introduced. As many of these unusual coins were brought home by servicemen who fought in Egypt during the

a) Great Britain 50p piece

b) China copper cash

c) Fiji penny   d) Iraq 10 fils

e) India   f) India 10 paise

44 Coins of unusual shapes

Second World War, they are still quite common in Britain and the Dominions.

India is another country which has experimented with several shapes for its coins. Bronze 1-pice coins issued during the 1940s had a hole so large that the coins looked like washers. Other Indian coins were square with rounded corners and coins with a scalloped edge have been in circulation for over seventy years. It would be possible to form an interesting collection of coins in unusual shapes (*Figure 44*).

Except for a very small number of shillings and florins dated before 1947 and still being used as 5p and 10p pieces, all the British coins now in circulation are made of either bronze or cupro-nickel. Only the pre-1947 'silver' coins contain any silver and although the little Maundy coins and a few of the large commemorative coins are made of silver, these are not intended for circulation. Years ago British coins were minted in copper, bronze, silver or gold. In other countries a much wider range of metals and materials has been used for coins.

In Russia during the early part of the 19th century some coins were made of platinum, a silvery-grey metal which is more expensive than gold. These Russian coins proved too expensive to produce, so the experiment was not repeated, but in times of war and economic difficulty many countries have been forced to save valuable metals such as gold and silver by using cheaper materials for their coins.

During the First World War and the years of hardship that followed it, Austria, Germany and Hungary were among the countries which issued coins made of iron. Germany also had coins made of aluminium and zinc. During the 1920s, when France was in financial difficulties, the French Mint made attractive coins from an alloy of aluminium and bronze, which gave them the appearance of gold, so that they occasionally deceive unwary collectors.

The Second World War brought many more coins in cheap metals. Even Sweden, which remained neutral during the war, was reduced to using iron for the low-value coins and billon, a mixture of silver and copper, for the high-value coins. A modern innovation in Sweden, Venezuela, the United States and a few other countries has been the introduction of coins made like a sandwich. Known as clad coins, these have a layer of one metal between two outer layers of a different metal. The United States, for example, has issued quarter-dollars, half-dollars and other coins made of a layer of copper between two layers of cupro-nickel. Venezuela has issued 5-centesimos coins of steel clad with outer layers of copper, while in Argentina there have been 1-peso coins also made of steel but clad with nickel.

Nickel is a highly satisfactory metal because it is so hard-wearing. France, the Netherlands and Switzerland are among the countries where nickel has been used for coins. Although American 5-cents coins are popularly known as 'nickels', they are made of an alloy containing 75% copper and only 25% nickel. The same alloy is used for the British decimal 5p, 10p and 50p coins. The drawback to using pure nickel is that because it is so hard it wears out the dies used for making the coins and replacing these adds to the expense of minting. The cupro-nickel alloy is not so hard and allows the dies a longer life.

In lonely islands and in under-developed countries people without the knowledge or the machinery for minting coins have often had to use other objects for their coinage. In the Fiji Islands whales' teeth were used for important transactions and a single tooth from a sperm whale was sufficient to buy a large canoe. In another Pacific Ocean country, the Solomon Islands, dogs' teeth were regarded as an acceptable currency, the two canine teeth from the upper jaw being the most valuable. Every reader of Wild West stories will know that the Red Indians used wampum as their coinage. Originally wampum was made from purple and white *Venus mercenaria* sea-shells threaded into patterns but after the arrival of Europeans coloured glass beads were also used. Contact with European traders gave the people of West Africa their currency of open-ended bracelets made from iron, copper or brass. These were known as manillas and eight or ten were the recognised price during the 16th century to buy an African slave. Most of the manillas used by British slave-traders were made in Birmingham. Much stranger was the currency used in Mongolia, Tibet and parts of Siberia until early in the 20th century. It consisted of tea-bricks made of pulverised scraps of tea-leaves mixed with ox-blood and formed into solid slabs. These were usually impressed with a pattern, a Russian letter or an inscription. An advantage of the tea-brick was that if its owner did not wish to spend it, he could chew it, make tea with it or use it for lighting a fire.

Coin dealers still occasionally offer Mongolian and Tibetan tea-bricks for sale, a typical price being about £25 for a brick measuring six inches by four inches. But few coin dealers are ever likely to have specimens of the currency used until recent times on the Pacific island of Yap. Known as 'fai', the coins of the Yap islanders were made of limestone quarried on another island about 400 miles away and brought to Yap by canoe. The fai were shaped like mill-stones, thick discs with a hole through the centre. The hole was useful for carrying the fai on a pole, because they varied in diameter from a few inches to ten feet or more. A small stone, weighing about ten or twelve pounds, would buy a pig or 500 coconuts but the large stones, weighing several tons, were seldom moved. When a man owned one, he let it stand at the door of his hut to show everyone how wealthy he was.

9
The Minor Marks
on a Coin

The artists who designed the beautiful coins of ancient Greece and engraved the dies for them were sometimes allowed to inscribe their names in the designs, just as a painter might add his or her name to a picture. Most of these Greek artists, indeed, are known to us only because their names are preserved on the coins they designed. In Roman times the moneyers were usually ordered to put on their coins the name or initials of the mint where these were being produced. This was not because the moneyers were considered to be talented artists but so that if any of the coins proved to be defective, perhaps too light in weight or too carelessly struck, the moneyer responsible could be traced and punished. This was certainly the reason why Anglo-Saxon, Norman and later monarchs insisted that their coins should bear the names of the moneyer and of the town where the mint was situated, usually in abbreviated form. During the autumn of 1124, for example, reports reached King Henry I that many poor people could not buy food for their families because market traders would not accept the badly struck and underweight silver pennies that were in circulation. Only people who were fortunate enough to have well-minted coins containing the full weight of silver could buy the food they needed. Furiously angry, the King ordered the Bishop of Salisbury to summon all the moneyers in England to assemble at Winchester during the Christmas season. When they arrived the Bishop's men-at-arms arrested and brutally punished all the moneyers responsible for producing the unsatisfactory coins. One account states that only three moneyers were acquitted but even if this is an exaggeration, the Assize of Moneyers, as it was called, must have been a terrible warning from the angry King. In modern times the initials of the artist who designs a coin and the initial letter of the mint where it is made are often included in the design. Sometimes the mint is identified by a small device such as a star, a pellet, a rosette, a crown or an acorn. Many Australian bronze coins made at the Perth Mint have a small pellet, described as a dot in Australian coin catalogues, after the words HALF PENNY or PENNY. Gold coins made at Perth, on the other hand, have the initial **P** just above the date on the reverse. Australian coins have sometimes been made at the Birmingham Mint and these have the mint-mark **H**, the initial of the founder of the company, Ralph Heaton (see Chapter 7). The letter **I** on other Australian coins shows that these have been made at one of the Indian mints, Bombay or Calcutta. The following list gives some of the mint-marks most likely to be found on modern coins.

A	Berlin, Paris *or* Vienna
B	Bombay *or* Brussels
C	Calcutta *or* Ottawa
CC	Carson City, U.S.A.
D	Denver, U.S.A., *or* Lyons
E	Edinburgh
F	Florence
G	Karlsruhe
H	Birmingham
I	Bombay *or* Calcutta
J	Hamburg
K	Bordeaux
KN	Kings Norton, Birmingham
L	Lahore, Lima *or* Lisbon
M	Melbourne *or* Milan
MD	Madrid
N	Naples
O	New Orleans, U.S.A.
P	Perth *or* Philadelphia, U.S.A.
R	Rome
S	Helsinki, San Francisco, U.S.A., *or* Sydney
SA	Pretoria
SOHO	Soho, Birmingham
T	Toledo *or* Turin
U	Stockholm
V	Valencia *or* Venice
Z	Grenoble *or* Zaragoza

Although moneyers no longer have their names on British coins, the artists who provide the designs are permitted to add their initials in an unobtrusive place. This may be on the truncation, the curved line at the base of the monarch's neck, or just below it, or on the reverse of the coin. The following list gives the names of some of the artists who have designed British and Commonwealth coins since the reign of King George III and whose initials may be found, with the help of a magnifying-glass, in their designs.

JB	James Berry (1906-1979)
JEB	Sir Joseph Boehm (1834-1890)
TB	Sir Thomas Brock (1847-1922)
SD	Stuart Devlin (1931-
EF	Edgar Fuller (1910-
KG	George Kruger Gray (1880-1943)
MG	Mary Gillick (1881-1965)
WG	William Gardner (1914-
K	Conrad Kuchler (c.1740-1810)
GL	Gilbert Ledward (1888-1960)
BM	Sir Bertram Mackennal (1863-1931)
JBM	Jean Baptiste Merlen (1769-1847)
PM	Percy Metcalfe (1895-1969)
BP	Benedetto Pistrucci (1784-1855)
HP	Thomas Humphrey Paget (1893-1974)
WP	Harold Wilson Parker (1896-
De S	George William de Saulles (1862-1903)
CT	Cecil Thomas (1885-1976)
LCW	Leonard Charles Wyon (1826-1891)
WW	William Wyon (1795-1851)

Although the date on a coin is not, strictly speaking, a minor mark, it may sometimes be puzzling. Holiday-makers and travellers visiting some of the North African countries, particularly Tunisia and Morocco, occasionally bring back coins which bear dates such as 1360 or 1371, suggesting that they were minted more than six hundred years ago. Yet the coins are in good condition, with little sign of wear, and their designs are distinctly modern in style.

The answer to the puzzle is that these coins are dated according to the Mohammedan calendar and not by the Christian calendar used in Britain and other western countries. Mohammed, the founder of the religion named after him, lived during the 7th century AD. In 622 he was forced by enemies who opposed his teaching to flee for his life from the Arabian city of Mecca, where he was living. He later returned in triumph to Mecca but his followers calculate their calendar from the date of his flight, which is known as the Hejira. An added complication is that the Mohammedans use the lunar year, reckoned from the phases of the Moon, instead of the solar year, reckoned from the length of time taken by the Earth to spin round the Sun. In Christian countries the calendar is based on the solar year, which is approximately 3% longer than the lunar year. A short sum is necessary to convert a Mohammedan date, known as AH, or the Year of the Hejira, into a Christian date. To convert AH 1371 into its AD equivalent, first subtract 3% of 1371, which to the nearest whole number is 41. This leaves 1330. Now add 622, and the result is 1952. This shows that a Moroccan coin dated AH 1371 was minted in 1952, and not six centuries ago, as at first appears. To avoid confusion, most Mohammedan countries now place both the Year of the Hejira and the Christian year on their coins.

One mistake sometimes made about the date on a commemorative coin, issued to mark a special event or anniversary, is to take the date of the event being commemorated as if it were the date when the coin itself was minted. An example of this can be seen on bronze pennies, known as 'twelfths of a shilling', issued in the Channel island of Jersey. On one side these have the inscription ISLAND OF JERSEY LIBERATED 1945 and some collectors have been puzzled because on the other side is the portrait of Queen Elizabeth II, who did not succeed to the throne until 1952.

The answer is simply that the coins were issued in 1954 to commemorate the liberation of the Channel Islands in 1945 from the German occupation during the Second World War.

10
Tokens
for Trade

The Civil War between King Charles I and his Parliament caused many difficulties for peaceful citizens as well as dangers for those who took part in it. One serious handicap was a chronic shortage of small change. The Royal Mint in the Tower of London and the various mints operated by the King's supporters in other cities were producing only gold or silver coins, which were too valuable to use in buying cheap goods. To overcome the shortage, merchants and tradesmen in many parts of the country began to issue their own farthings and halfpennies.

Known as tokens, these private coins were usually made of copper or brass and they gave rise to the expression 'not worth a brass farthing' to describe something which is practically worthless. The tokens were usually inscribed with the name of the person who issued them, his occupation, and the name of the town where he lived. There would also be a device showing his trade or the crest of the company or trade guild to which he belonged. In some towns the local corporation issued its own tokens.

Altogether about ten thousand merchants, tradesmen and corporations issued tokens between 1648 and 1672. In Wiltshire, for example, more than fifty towns and villages were provided with tokens by local citizens. The widest choice was to be found in Salisbury, where almost sixty different tokens were issued. One design bore the name of Edward Faulconer, who was a skinner, with the coat-of arms of the Skinners' Guild, of which he was a member. Bakers often chose wheat-sheaves for the device on their tokens while butchers usually favoured a meat cleaver. Most of the tokens were circular, like ordinary coins, but others were square and some were even heart-shaped. One of the last, issued in Chester, was inscribed 'Thomas Cotton of Middlewich, his halfpenny. Although but brass yet let me pass, 1669'.

As well as being useful for giving change to customers, the tokens also made a handsome profit for the tradesmen who issued them. The farthings could be bought from the manufacturers at about five for a penny but they passed into circulation at the rate of four for a penny, so that on every pennyworth of tokens the tradesman made one farthing profit. Normally the tradesman would exchange the tokens, in sufficient quantity, for silver coins of the realm, at the rate of a silver threepence for twelve tokens or a shilling for 48 tokens. Any tokens not exchanged in this way also represented extra profit for the tradesman. Many must have been lost or mislaid, for examples are still quite common, although most of the surviving tokens are badly worn. Prices vary between about £3 and £5 for tokens in fine condition but rare specimens and those in extremely fine condition are more expensive. In 1672 King Charles II issued a royal proclamation announcing the introduction of new regal farthings and halfpennies, and declaring the private tokens to be illegal.

By delving into old records in local public libraries it is often possible to discover more about the life and work of the tradesmen who issued these 17th century tokens. The Salisbury skinner, Edward Faulconer, for example, became the mayor of Salisbury in 1686 and was one of the eighty voters who had the right to elect Salisbury's two members of parliament.

The next period when a shortage of small change prompted private citizens and companies to issue their own coins came towards the end of the 18th century. The shortage this time was not due to a civil war but to the increase in trade and commerce resulting from the Industrial Revolution. Many people who had once worked as farm-labourers and had received part of their wages in the form of food or firewood, moved to the growing towns to work in the new factories. Here their wages could be paid only in cash. The Royal Mint was again neglecting to produce copper coins for small change, so companies and tradesmen again began issuing their own token coins. Most of these were halfpennies or pennies and they were generally much more artistically designed and better made than the 17th century tokens.

The first of the new tokens were issued in 1787 by the Parys Mine Company, which had copper mines at Parys, in Anglesey, and smelting-works at Swansea, Birmingham and other places. Some of the manillas, the bracelets used as currency in West Africa, were made by the Parys Copper Company. For the design of the tokens the company chose a bearded portrait of a Druid surrounded by a wreath of oakleaves and acorns. The Druid, one of the priests of the Celtic people who were living in Britain when the Romans came, was chosen because Anglesey is traditionally said to have been the last stronghold of the Druids and their followers. The oak-tree and the mistletoe were sacred to the Druids. On the reverse of the tokens was a monogram of the company's initials, P.M.C., and an inscription, continued round the edge of the token, stating WE PROMISE TO PAY THE BEARER ONE PENNY ON DEMAND IN LONDON, LIVERPOOL OR ANGLESEY. This meant that anyone taking the tokens to the company's offices at those places could exchange them for regal coins.

Altogether more than 300 tons of copper were used for making the Druid's Head halfpennies and pennies. Many dies had to be used, so there were many slight variations in the design. The tokens were the first copper pennies to be used in Britain and they were so popular that other companies quickly followed the example. Most of the new tokens were made in Birmingham, some by Matthew Boulton at Soho, and they were soon circulating in all the industrial districts. Unfortunately, because the tokens were unofficial and not protected by the law, unscrupulous people were free to make imitation tokens which they had no intention of exchanging for proper coins. Other companies issued tokens simply to advertise the goods they had for sale and coin dealers even ordered series of tokens in attractive designs to sell to collectors (*Figures 45 & 46*).

The designs, indeed, were many and varied. Some showed views of buildings in the towns where they were issued, others featured the town coat-of-arms, and some portrayed Britannia or the lady who personified Ireland, Hibernia. Among the celebrities whose portraits appeared on tokens were William Shakespeare, the actor David Garrick and the prime minister, William Pitt. One wealthy iron-master, John Wilkinson, put his own portrait on the many tokens he issued to pay the workpeople in his iron foundries at Bilston, Bersham, near Wrexham, and Willey, in Shropshire. After Britain went to war with France in 1793, the tokens began to reflect patriotic sentiments by depicting warships and soldiers. Room was found on them for such rousing inscriptions as PROSPERITY TO

45 Tradesmen's tokens. A collection of coins made by the tradesmen of Northampton

THE WOODEN WALLS OF OLD ENGLAND and ENGLISH LIBERTY PRESERVED BY VIRTUE AND COURAGE.

Examples of these tokens are still plentiful, though most are in worn condition. It is possible to form an interesting collection of the tokens issued in almost any large British city or industrial

46 Manchester ½d. token dated 1793 (*obverse & reverse*)

district. Research in local libraries may reveal the historical background to the various issues.

After Matthew Boulton had begun producing his fine new copper coins, the cartwheel pennies and twopences in 1797 and the slightly smaller pennies, halfpennies and farthings between 1799 and 1807, the need for the private tokens diminished and they ceased to appear. But the long war against France dragged on and the prices of many commodities required for the army and navy, among them copper, began rising steadily. Eventually Matthew Boulton's copper coins were being hoarded and melted down for their metal. By 1810 the shortage of small change, both copper and silver coins, was as severe as it had been in 1787. Again companies and tradesmen were forced to issue their own tokens. Most were dated 1811 or 1812 but in Birmingham a huge copper threepenny token was issued in 1813.

The designs of these 19th century tokens were even more patriotic in sentiment than those of the earlier issues. Many had portraits of King George III, Lord Nelson and the Duke of Wellington. It was a sign of the times, too, that paper money was offered for the tokens instead of gold or silver coins. ONE POUND NOTE PAYABLE FOR 240 TOKENS was a common inscription.

People were by now becoming tired of using such a mixture of tokens and regal coins, especially when many of the tokens were worthless imitations which could not be exchanged for genuine coins or banknotes. Eventually Parliament passed an act declaring that from 1 January 1818 the issue and circulation of private coins would be illegal. Three years later the Royal Mint began producing adequate quantities of small copper coins and there has never since then been a national shortage of small change. Many tradesmen during Queen Victoria's reign issued brass or copper tokens but these were for advertising purposes only and were not to be used as coins.

11
Some Curious
Coins

CUMBERLAND JACKS

Among the unusual coins sometimes found in trinket-boxes, the drawers of old cupboards and even in dealers' trays are small brass medalets with a portrait of the young Queen Victoria on one side and the picture of a horseman on the other. At first glance the horseman might be taken for St. George, who is portrayed on the reverse of many British gold coins, but closer examination shows that above his head are the words TO HANOVER. These medalets are known as Cumberland Jacks (*Figure 47*).

In certain European countries there was, until recent years, a law preventing any woman from becoming the ruling monarch. The Salic Law, as it was called, dated from the time when a king was expected to lead his army into battle, a duty for which a woman was considered unfitted. After King George I had come from Hanover in 1714 to take the British throne, his German territories became part of the British dominions. But in 1837, when Queen Victoria succeeded to the throne, she could not rule in Hanover, so her nearest male relative, her uncle the Duke of Cumberland, went to become King of Hanover instead.

47 Cumberland Jack

The Duke was detested in Britain, partly for his autocratic political views and partly because he was widely suspected of having murdered his valet. The brass medalets bearing his portrait on the reverse were issued by some of his political opponents to express their delight at his departure 'To Hanover'. On some of the medalets he is clearly shown to have a monkey's head. It is only fair to record that the Duke proved to be a wise and capable King of Hanover, as much respected by his German subjects as he had been hated in Britain.

FRACTIONAL FARTHINGS

After years of inflation in Britain the bronze farthings would buy so little that after 1956 no more were minted. Four of them were worth a pre-decimal penny but it would take about ten of them to make a decimal penny, so that today a farthing would be a useless coin. Yet for many years the Royal Mint produced not only farthings but even tinier coins, half-farthings, third-farthings and quarter-farthings. These were so small and of so little value that many were saved as curiosities and examples still occasionally come to light.

The fractional farthings, as they are called, were not intended for circulation in Britain and only the half-farthing was recognised as legal tender in the United Kingdom. It was first minted in 1828 for use in Ceylon, now Sri Lanka, which had recently become a British possession. Ceylon was using a mixture of Dutch, Indian and British coins, and the half-farthings were to be rated as one-twelfth of an Indian anna, then worth three-halfpence. Although there was no pressing need for such a coin in Britain, the half-farthing was declared to be legal tender in 1842 but no more were minted after 1856.

The third-farthings were first issued in 1827 for use in Malta, also a new British possession, where it was intended to replace a little local copper coin, the grano. The third-farthings were useful for buying small quantities of fruit, nuts or vegetables and they were minted at intervals until 1913. Those with the portrait of King Edward VII or King George V can still be bought for about 50p in fine condition.

The quarter-farthings were intended as part of the coinage in

Ceylon, two of them making a half-farthing. They were issued only between 1839 and 1853, so they are much scarcer than the other fractional farthings, costing several pounds in fine condition and much more if showing little sign of wear. It is strange to think that a visitor to Ceylon in 1853 could have obtained 192 quarter-farthings for a British shilling. Today the same number of the little copper coins in **FDC** condition would be worth about £4,000.

Mention must also be made of another tiny coin minted between 1834 and 1862 for use in British colonies overseas. This was the silver 1½d, which was specially designed for circulation in Ceylon, British Guiana, now Guyana, and the British West Indies, where at that time ordinary British coins were used. Quite large numbers were minted so the silver 1½d coins are still common in worn condition but a specimen in **FDC** condition would cost at least £10.

GOOD OLD GUINEAS

Coin collectors are sometimes puzzled by small coin-like medalets which have a portrait of King George III on the obverse and the royal coat-of-arms in a spade-shaped shield on the reverse. Made of brass, these medalets are obviously imitations of the gold spade guineas but they are puzzling because their inscription consists of a long string of apparently meaningless initials and abbreviations instead of the King's titles, as on the genuine guineas (*Figure 48*).

The medalets were issued in Victorian times and well into the 20th century for use as counters in card games or for children to use when playing with the large dolls' houses which were so popular years ago. So that the manufacturers could not be accused of counterfeiting the gold guineas in order to defraud unwary people, they deliberately changed the inscriptions. But these are not entirely meaningless, for they give clues to the names of the manufacturers themselves. The inscription B. BROS REX F.D. CLXX. HOCKLEY. B.I.R.M., for example, means that the medalet was made by Bancroft Brothers, 170 Hockley Street, Birmingham. An even longer inscription, G.Y.I. ET F.G. REX S. UF. ST. DS. T. M. S. ET., shows the medalet bearing it was made by another Birmingham firm, George Yorke Iliffe and Frederick Gardner, Suffolk Street, die-sinkers, tool-makers, stampers, etc.

Sometimes the medalets have a false date such as 1701, long

48 'Good Old Days' imitation guinea

before George III was born. Others have short advertisements for tradesmen, among them J. SAINSBURY, PROVISION MERCHANT, OPPOSITE WEST CROYDON STATION, or A. FATTORINI AND SONS, WHOLESALE JEWELLERS, BRADFORD. Some even have the words IN MEMORY OF THE GOOD OLD DAYS, so that collectors jokingly refer to them as 'the Good Old Guineas!' They were sold by the manufacturers at a few pence per hundred and they are still very common. To a coin collector they are simply interesting curiosities.

HOLEY DOLLARS

The early British settlers in Australia took few coins with them and as the Royal Mint in London was not providing sufficient coins for Britain itself, there was little likelihood of its sparing any for the far-away Australian colonies. As a result, the settlers used any coins they could obtain from ships that called. Barter was also widely practised, rum being the most popular commodity for buying and selling. In 1814 Governor Macquarie of New South Wales tried to alleviate the shortage of coins by issuing what became known as 'holey dollars' and 'dumps'. The British government had sent to the colony a consignment of 40,000 Spanish silver dollars, or 'pieces of eight' as they were called. These were well-known and useful coins, acceptable almost anywhere in the world. Governor Macquarie realised that if he issued them, they would soon be used to buy goods from ships' crews and would then be taken away from the colony. He therefore ordered that the centre of each dollar should be punched out, leaving a ring like a washer. On each ring was over-stamped a new inscription, NEW SOUTH

WALES 1813 - FIVE SHILLINGS, and this was to be the value of the holey dollar.

The dump, the circular piece of silver from the centre of the dollar, was not wasted. The original Spanish design was smoothed away and replaced by a new design. This consisted of a crown surrounded by the inscription NEW SOUTH WALES 1813. On the other side was the new value, FIFTEEN PENCE. This ingenious scheme mutilated the dollars, so that they would be of little value outside New South Wales. At the same time it provided 80,000 useful silver coins and gave Australians their first distinctive coinage. Most satisfactory of all, because each dollar had cost only five shillings before being turned into two coins with a total value of 6s. 3d, Governor Macquarie made a profit for his government of 1s. 3d on every dollar.

LUNDY PUFFINS

The island of Lundy, which lies in the Bristol Channel about twelve miles from the coast of Devon, derives its name from an old word, *lund*, meaning a puffin. These attractive sea-birds still nest on Lundy and they are often featured on picture postcards and china ornaments bought by the holiday-makers who visit the island.

During the 1920s Lundy was owned by a London businessman, Martin Coles Harman, and in 1929 he decided to issue special coins partly to use in the shop he ran on Lundy and partly as souvenirs for visitors. From the Birmingham Mint he ordered coins showing his name, his own portrait and the date, 1929, on one side. On the other was a picture of a puffin, the name LUNDY and a value in the currency he had chosen, ONE PUFFIN or HALF PUFFIN. The coins were made of bronze and in size were roughly the same as the ordinary penny and halfpenny of that time.

Unfortunately for Mr. Harman, he was breaking the law by issuing in the United Kingdom 'a piece of metal as a token for money'. He was taken to the magistrates' court at Bideford and fined five pounds for issuing the tokens and his appeal against the sentence was later dismissed by the King's Bench court, in London. Harman had obtained 50,000 of each of the two coins and many were later bought by dealers. They are still occasionally offered for sale, usually in **FDC** condition, at about £2 each.

MAUNDY MONEY

The little silver 1p, 2p, 3p and 4p coins known as Maundy money have already been mentioned several times. Because they are so popular with collectors, some details of their history may be interesting. The day before Jesus Christ was crucified he gathered his disciples in a room at Jerusalem for their Last Supper together. Before they began their meal Jesus washed the feet of the disciples and gave them a command, that they should love and care for one another in the same way. From the Latin word *mandatum*, meaning 'a command', the day is known in the Christian calendar as Maundy Thursday.

Since very early times there have been ceremonies on Maundy Thursday at which Christians have celebrated Christ's command by giving food, clothing and money to poor people. The first English monarch recorded as having attended a Maundy ceremony was King John, who distributed silver pennies to poor men at Rochester Cathedral in 1213. Some monarchs have also washed the feet of poor people, as Jesus had done, but King William III seems to have been the last to do so. In 1582 Queen Elizabeth I presented to 48 poor women 'fortie-eight pence in memorye of Her Majestie's age'. This connection between the monarch's age and the amount of Maundy money presented to the poor has continued ever since.

The practice of giving food and clothing was discontinued during Queen Victoria's reign and the distribution of the Maundy money was for many years left to a court official, the Lord High Almoner. In 1932 King George V became the first monarch for almost 250 years to attend the Maundy ceremony in person. Since then the monarch has usually taken part. Queen Elizabeth II has broken with precedent by holding the ceremony in churches or cathedrals in many parts of the country instead of only in the traditional place, Westminster Abbey.

The recipients of the Maundy money are carefully chosen from elderly local men and women of good character who have been active in voluntary work for the church or the community. The coins, made of sterling silver, are legal tender and can be spent as ordinary coins but there are so many collectors wishing to buy them that they are worth more than their face value. Sets of the four Queen Victoria coins minted during the last years of her reign now cost about £30 or £35 in FDC condition. Those of Queen Elizabeth II are more expensive, costing about £45 or £50, but single coins from earlier reigns, as far back as the Stuarts, may be bought for a pound or two each if the coin has been in circulation and shows signs of wear and tear.

EDWARD VIII COINS

The short reign of King Edward VIII ended before the Royal Mint could put the coins bearing his portrait into circulation in Britain or the British dominions. But some new coins bearing his name, though not his portrait, had already been issued before the King abdicated in December 1936. In British East Africa, British West Africa, Fiji and New Guinea the low value coins had a hole through the centre, so that they did not bear the portrait of the reigning monarch. Instead they simply had a crown, the royal monogram and titles, and the date. For the new Edward VIII coins the monogram was E.R.I., standing for Edwardus, Rex Imperator, or Edward, King Emperor, and the date was 1936.

As they had no portrait these coins could be designed and minted easily and quickly, so there was time for them to be issued before the King announced his intention of abdicating. Some of the coins for East and West Africa were made by the Birmingham Mint and Imperial Metal Industries, and have the mint-marks **H** or **KN** in their design. People seeing these colonial coins with the monogram and titles of King Edward VIII assume that they are valuable, especially since the few brass threepences minted for him, which escaped into circulation, are very rare indeed. But most of the colonial coins were minted in large numbers and are still quite common. The scarcest are the Fiji pennies, of which 120,000 were minted, and the New Guinea pennies, of which 360,000 were minted at the Melbourne Mint, Australia. The other coins are sold by dealers at between £1 and £3 each in first class condition, the Fiji and New Guinea coins being more expensive.

12
Some Famous
Foreign Coins

CHINESE CASH

Although historians generally agree that the first coins were minted in the kingdom of Lydia, in Asia Minor, about the middle of the 7th century BC, coins were certainly being used in China very soon afterwards. Even more remarkable is the fact that the designs of some of these Chinese coins remained virtually unchanged from 6th century BC to the early years of the 20th century, a span of about 2,500 years.

Known to the Chinese as ch'ien and to foreigners as cash, the coins were made of brass or copper. They were circular and quite thin, with a raised rim to protect the designs from wear. There were no portraits or pictures on the cash but each bore an inscription in Chinese characters giving the name of the emperor for whom it was issued or of the place where it was minted, as well as its face value. Sometimes the coins also had political slogans such as 'Coin of Coming Prosperity' or 'Coin of United Law and Order'. Every coin had a large square hole through the centre (*Illustrated on page 74*).

At first the cash were made in various sizes and circulated with the other coins made in the shape of miniature knives and spades. During the reign of the Emperor Shih Huang Ti, who began building the Great Wall of China about 220 BC, the cash were standardised in size and weight. Later emperors reduced the size but the general design remained unchanged. The last cash were minted about seventy years ago.

JOACHIMSTALERS

Early in the 16th century a Czech nobleman, the Count of Schlik,

discovered that there were large deposits of silver ore on his estate
at Joachimstal, in the Bohemian mountains. He decided to use the
silver for minting large coins which would be accepted by merchants and tradesmen throughout central Europe. First issued in
1520, the coins measured 40 mms in diameter. On one side they had
a portrait of St. Joachim, known in English as St. Joseph, and on
the other a rampant lion, still the emblem of Czechoslovakia. Other
noblemen were issuing large silver coins in different designs but
these were far out-numbered by the coins being minted at
Joachimstal.

The Count of Schlik became very wealthy but the success of his
enterprise aroused the envy of his overlord, the King of Bohemia.
In 1528 the King took possession of the mines and the mint, and
production of the coins was rapidly increased. Because so many
came from Joachimstal, all the large silver coins became known as
joachimstalers. The name was soon abbreviated to talers, and from
this were derived the many other names given to large silver coins
of this type.

In Germany and Austria they were known as thalers, in the
Netherlands as daalers, and in Denmark and Sweden as dalers.
From this it was only a short step to the word dollars, now used for
the basic unit of coinage in many countries throughout the world.
Unlike their ancestor, the joachimstaler of 1520, very few of the
modern dollars are made of silver.

PIECES OF EIGHT

At the end of Robert Louis Stevenson's popular adventure story of
Treasure Island, young Jim Hawkins confesses that sometimes in
nightmares he hears the shrill voice of Long John Silver's green
parrot shrieking: 'Pieces of eight! Pieces of eight!' Jim Hawkins
and Long John Silver are only fictional characters but many
thousands of actual people, both pirates and honest citizens, must
have lost their lives in the quest for these historic Spanish coins.

The name pieces of eight was given to the coins because they were
worth eight reales. The real was a silver coin about the same size as
a British sixpence, so a piece of eight was similar in size to a British
crown and worth only a little less. There were many types of the
pieces of eight, some with the portraits of the monarchs who ruled

Spain and the Spanish colonies of Central and South America from the early 15th to the 19th century.

The best known type was the pillar dollar, so called because on one side it showed two tall pillars draped in ribbons and topped by a crown. These represented the twin rocks which stand at the Spanish entrance to the Mediterranean and which are known as the Pillars of Hercules because the legendary strong man is said to have placed them there. On the other side the pillar dollars had the Spanish royal coat-of-arms and a Latin inscription proudly proclaiming the Spanish monarch to be 'By the Grace of God, King of Spain and the Indies'.

The early pieces of eight were very crudely minted from blanks roughly cut from bars of silver, but during the 18th century mints were opened in the Spanish colonies of Mexico, Guatemala, Peru, Colombia and Chile. Here the coins were well minted in huge quantities and they were soon eagerly accepted throughout the Mediterranean and the Americas. Certainly no story of the Spanish Main would be complete without its treasure of glittering silver pieces of eight! (*Figures 49 & 50*).

MARIA THERESA

Although she died two hundred years ago, the Austrian Empress Maria Theresa is still being portrayed on coins produced at the Austrian state mint in Vienna. The coins are known as thalers, a German word from which the name dollar is derived. They are the same size as a British crown piece and contain more than an ounce of good quality silver.

Maria Theresa succeeded to the Austrian throne in 1740 and reigned for forty years. During that time several different designs were used for the thalers, the portrait being altered to show that the Empress was growing older. On the reverse was the Austrian imperial coat-of-arms. Because of its impressive appearance and the value of the silver in it, Austrians trading with eastern countries found that the thaler was very popular. Even in distant African and Asian countries, native traders were happy to accept the handsome coins in exchange for their silks and spices, ivory and ebony. Arab girls saved the thalers for their wedding dowries and slave-traders paid in thalers for the poor wretches they bought in the slave markets.

49 Spanish piece of eight, minted in Peru, showing pillars representing the twin rocks at the entrance to the Mediterranean

50 Spanish 8 realès piece, showing pillars and countermarked with head of George III

Maria Theresa died in 1780 but the demand for the thalers continued unabated. In 1867 King Theodore of Abyssinia imprisoned and ill-treated some British subjects in his fortress of Magdala. To finance an expedition to release them the British government purchased half a million thalers at a cost of £115,000 and raised income tax by one penny in the pound to pay for them.

When the Italian dictator Mussolini was preparing to invade Abyssinia in 1935, he persuaded the Austrian government to allow Italy to mint some Maria Theresa thalers to pay for his invasion. To prevent Italy from having a monopoly of the useful coins, other European countries, including Britain, also began to mint the thalers. After the Second World War Italy, Britain and the other countries agreed to cease minting the coins on the understanding that the Vienna Mint would provide adequate supplies at a reasonable price. Today the Maria Theresa thalers are produced mainly for sale to coin collectors. They are still dated 1780 and they still bear the Latin inscription announcing that the elderly lady portrayed on them is 'By the Grace of God, Roman Empress, Queen of Hungary and Bohemia, Archduchess of Austria, Duchess of Burgundy and Countess of the Tyrol'.

AMERICAN DOLLARS

When the British Colonies in North America had won their independence as the United States, they were faced with the task of providing a coinage of their own. Until then they had been using a mixture of English, French and Spanish coins, of which the English shillings and the Spanish pieces of eight were the most useful. In 1792 Congress agreed to introduce a new silver coin similar to the Spanish piece of eight. It was to have a portrait of a woman personifying Liberty on one side and the American eagle on the other, and it was to be called a dollar.

The first American dollars were minted in 1794 at the new mint in Philadelphia. A few years later they were discontinued for a time while the mint concentrated on smaller coins, copper cents and silver quarter and half dollars. In 1878 a different portrait of Liberty was introduced. This was designed by a British engraver, George Morgan, who had been trained at the Royal Mint in London. Using a Philadelphia school teacher as his model, Morgan portrayed Liberty with long hair and wearing a wreath of wheat and cotton. Known as the Morgan dollars, these handsome coins were minted in large numbers until 1904 and again in 1921. In that year they were replaced by dollars in a new design showing Liberty with a spiked head-dress representing the rising Sun.

The 1921 dollars were intended to commemorate the return of peace after the First World War, and are usually known as the Peace dollars. They were minted regularly until 1935, when the high cost of silver made them too expensive to produce.

In 1971, to honour President Eisenhower and to commemorate the first landing of American astronauts on the Moon, dollars bearing the President's portrait were introduced. They were issued regularly until 1978 but with several different reverse designs. Most of the Eisenhower dollars were clad coins, made like sandwiches of copper, nickel or silver.

In 1979 yet another type of dollar was issued. It honours an American woman, Susan B. Anthony (1820-1906), who spent her life in campaigning for women to be granted the right to vote and given better conditions at work. The Susan Anthony dollar is much smaller than previous issues and is made of cupro-nickel. It is intended to replace the dollar banknote.

Glossary

BLANK The piece of metal before the design is struck on it.

BRITANNIA GROAT The silver fourpence minted between 1836 and 1855 (and again in 1888 for use in British Guiana), so called because the reverse featured Britannia.

BULL HEAD COINS The halfcrowns minted for George III in 1816 and 1817, so called from the heavy features and thick bull-like neck of the portrait.

BUN HEAD COINS The bronze coins minted for Queen Victoria between 1860 and 1894 (1895 for the farthings).

CARTWHEEL COINS The large copper pennies and twopences minted by Matthew Boulton in 1797.

COUNTERMARK A mark stamped on a coin, usually to alter its value.

DOUBLE FLORIN The silver four-shilling piece minted for Queen Victoria between 1887 and 1890.

EXERGUE The space below the main feature of the design, usually occupied by the date.

GODLESS FLORIN The 1849 florin, so called because the inscription DEI GRATIA (By the Grace of God) was omitted from the design. Replaced in 1851 by a new design with the abbreviation D.G. restored. Also known as the *Graceless Florin*.

HIBERNIA The personification of Ireland, shown on Irish coins as a lady seated with a harp at her side.

JUBILEE COINAGE The gold and silver coins minted between 1887 and 1892 to commemorate Queen Victoria's golden jubilee.

LEGEND The old-fashioned term for the inscription on a coin.

MEDALET A small medal resembling a coin but having no face value and not intended to be used as money.

MINT-MARK The mark on a coin, usually initials or a small device such as a star, a heart, a bell or a scallop shell, which shows where the coin was minted.

MULE A coin produced when the moneyer has accidentally used dies intended for two different coins, so that the obverse and the reverse do not match.

NUMISMATICS The collection and study of coins (from a Greek word *nomisma*, meaning a coin).

OBVERSE The front or 'heads' side of a coin, bearing the more important design.

PATINA The coating, usually green or brown, on old copper and bronze coins, protecting them from corrosion.

PILE The lower die in hammered coinage, usually with the design of the obverse.

REVERSE The back or 'tails' side of a coin.

SALTIRE An X-shaped cross, usually known as St. Andrew's Cross.

SPADE GUINEA The guinea minted for George III between 1787 and 1799, so called because the shield on the reverse resembled the spades in a pack of playing cards.

TRADE DOLLAR A large silver coin issued between 1895 and 1935 for use in the Far East. The obverse featured a standing figure of Britannia. Most of the trade dollars were minted at branches of the Royal Mint in Calcutta and Bombay.

TRUNCATION The place where the portrait on a coin is cut off, usually in a curved line at the base of the neck or below the shoulders.

TRUSSEL The upper die in hammered coinage, usually with the design of the reverse.

VEILED HEAD The portrait of Queen Victoria on the last coins of her reign, introduced in 1893.

YOUNG HEAD The portrait used on most of the early coins of Queen Victoria. She is bare-headed, with her hair gathered high at the back and held in place by two ribbons.

For Further Reading

There is no single volume in which all the coins minted during the past 2,000 years are listed and priced. Instead the coin collector has to be content with catalogues listing the coins of individual countries. The following are useful and others should be available in the local public library. Coin dealers may also be able to recommend suitable books and a list of newly published books appears annually in *Coin Year Book* (Numismatic Publishing Co.).

Roman Coins and their Values by David R. Sear (B.A. Seaby Ltd.)

Standard Catalogue of British Coins, Parts 1 and 2 - England and the United Kingdom by Peter Seaby (B.A. Seaby Ltd.)

British Tokens and their Values by Peter Seaby and Monica Bussell (B.A. Seaby Ltd.)

Coins and Tokens of Scotland by P. Frank Purvey (B.A. Seaby Ltd.)

Coins and Tokens of Ireland by P. Seaby (B.A. Seaby Ltd.)

Guide Book of United States Coins by R.S. Yeoman (Western Publishing Co., Racine, Wisconsin, U.S.A.)

World Coin Catalogue: Twentieth Century by Gunter Schon (Barrie and Jenkins Ltd.)

Catalogue of the World's Most Popular Coins by Fred Reinfeld and Burton Hobson (Oak Tree Press Ltd.)

Current Coins of the World - Since 1950 by R.S. Yeoman (Western Publishing Co., Racine, Wisconsin, U.S.A.)

Dictionary of Numismatic Names by Albert R. Frey (Spink and Son Ltd.)

Index